TRUE PARADOX

HOW CHRISTIANITY
MAKES SENSE OF OUR
COMPLEX WORLD

DAVID SKEEL

IVP Books

An imprint of InterVarsity Press
Downers Grove, Illinois

InterVarsity Press
P.O. Box 1400, Downers Grove, IL 60515-1426
World Wide Web: www.ivpress.com
Email: email@ivpress.com

InterVarsity Press® is the book-publishing division of InterVarsity Christian Fellowship/USA®, a movement
of students and faculty active on campus at hundreds of universities, colleges and schools of nursing in the
United States of America, and a member movement of the International Fellowship of Evangelical Students.
For information about local and regional activities visit intervarsity.org.

Scripture quotations, unless otherwise noted, are from The Holy Bible, English Standard Version, copyright
© 2001 by Crossway Bibles, a division of Good News Publishers. Used by permission. All rights reserved.

While all stories in this book are true, some names and identifying information in this book have been changed
to protect the privacy of the individuals involved.

Dedication page artwork: ©2010 by Melissa Gilstrap. Used by permission. All rights reserved.

Cover design: David Fassett
Interior design: Beth McGill
Images: © oanav/iStockphoto

ISBN 978-0-8308-3676-5 (print)
ISBN 978-0-8308-9669-1 (digital)

Printed in the United States of America ∞

Library of Congress Cataloging-in-Publication Data

Skeel, David A., Jr., 1961-
   True paradox : how Christianity makes sense of our complex world / David Skeel.
      pages cm
   Includes bibliographical references.
   ISBN 978-0-8308-3676-5 (pbk. : alk. paper)
   1. Christian philosophy. I. Title.
   BR100.S525 2014
   230—dc23

                                                                                            2014022822

P 21 20 19 18 17 16 15 14 13 12 11 10 9 8 7 6 5 4 3 2

Y 32 31 30 29 28 27 26 25 24 23 22 21 20 19 18 17 16 15 14

For Bill

CONTENTS

PREFACE

A few months after this book first began to take shape, I mentioned to a Christian friend that I was writing a short book defending Christianity. Her reaction was enthusiastic and expectant. "I sure hope it's simple!" she gushed. "What we need are books that explain the simple truths of Christianity. Is it simple?"

I wasn't quite sure how to respond. "Not exactly," I finally said, borrowing my words from a rental car ad of several decades ago. The core truths of Christianity are indeed simple. And I don't think most readers will find the book difficult to read. But this is not a book about the simplicity of Christianity. My theme is Christianity and complexity.

Complexity is widely seen as an embarrassment for Christianity. How can an ancient religion like Christianity possibly begin to explain a world that is as complex as we now know our world to be? After all, Christianity arose at a time when the sun was thought to revolve around the earth, modern travel and warfare were unimaginable, and no one dreamed of the secret life of subatomic particles. An atheist scientist friend of mine recently remarked that Christianity appears to be "not much more than a human creation of Bronze Age peasants derived from wholly unexceptional and largely fictional narratives." Although the friend is not hostile to Christianity (or me), he is convinced that the world long ago passed Christianity by.

The assumption that Christianity and complexity don't mix seems to be shared not just by religious skeptics, but also by many Christians. Yet it actually gets things precisely backward. Complexity is not an embarrassment for Christianity; it is Christianity's natural element. Or so I will try to persuade you from this page of *True Paradox* to the last.

The complexities that will concern us most arise from the intangible aspects of our experience. Why do we have consciousness— and odder yet, why do we have a compulsion to devise elaborate ideas about our place in the universe? Why do we experience beauty as transcendent yet somehow impermanent and corrupted, and suffering as somehow wrong, rather than simply a part of the natural order? Why do the advocates of each new system of justice believe they can devise legal codes that will achieve a fully just social order, even though every previous system of justice has failed? These are the kinds of questions that any religion or system of thought that claims to be true needs to have good answers to.

The questions we will be considering are, in a sense, a prequel to conventional Christian apologetics—that is, defenses of Christianity, usually aimed at those who are already intrigued by Christianity. (I suppose that makes these opening words a preface to a preface.) My hope is that at least a few people who don't think there's any reason to take Christianity seriously when they pick up this book or who are harboring doubts about their Christian faith will be tempted to read much better (and longer) books of conventional apologetics, such as C. S. Lewis's *Mere Christianity* or Timothy Keller's *The Reason for God*. I like to imagine this book as a bit like a gateway drug—a gateway to a faith that has little in common with the opiate Karl Marx so famously imagined.

■ ■ ■

Every book is shaped by its author's perspective, whether the author admits it or not, and that is perhaps especially true with a book like this one. So let me make a few very basic confessions. I have been a law professor for nearly twenty-five years, after—among other adventures—studying literature and zoology in college and practicing law for several years in a large Philadelphia law firm. I came late to Christianity—embracing it first at the end of my college years—and I still remember the questions that troubled me and what it felt like to discover that Christianity is not simply a lifeless list of rules.

■ ■ ■

In the course of this work, I will range broadly (and often very briefly) across religions and systems of thought, from Immanuel Kant and John Stuart Mill to pantheist and dualist religions. It will suffice to define nearly all of these thinkers and ideas when they first appear in the discussion. But the two most frequently discussed perspectives should be briefly explained here.

The first is Christianity, of course. What do I mean by "Christian"? For my purposes, a Christian is a man or woman (or girl or boy) who genuinely believes that Jesus Christ is God, that he was resurrected from the dead and that he is our means of reconciliation with God. The heart of Christianity lies in these (simple) beliefs, which can be summarized as belief in Jesus' resurrection. As the apostle Paul says of himself and his fellow Christians, "If Christ has not been raised, then our preaching is in vain and your faith is in vain" (1 Corinthians 15:14).

Some might complain that this definition leaves out too much. A true Christian, they might argue, also believes that Adam and Eve were actual people, not simply characters in a story; that the Exodus took place as described in the Bible; and that the four Gospels are an accurate historical account of Jesus' life and ministry. I would not for a moment suggest that these or a number of other issues are unimportant. But they do not lie at the very heart of Christianity. The feature that makes Christianity different from any other religion or system of thought is Christians' belief that Jesus, the God who became man, suffered, died and was raised from the dead to reconcile humans with God.

I give the same answer to those who might criticize my definition as too stringent. In his lovely meditation on embracing Christianity, *My Bright Abyss*, the poet Christian Wiman says, "I'm a Christian not because of the resurrection (I wrestle with this)," before marveling that Christ's suffering "shatters the iron walls around individual human suffering" and "makes extreme human compassion—to the point of death, even—possible."[1] But to say that the core of Christianity is human compassion robs this faith of its transformative potential. The resurrection is not one particular doctrine that we can agree to disagree about; it is the mysterious source of a new way of living. Wiman himself later comes to the same conclusion, acknowledging that "to be a Christian has to mean believing in the resurrected Christ."[2]

Christians do hold other beliefs as well, some of which will figure prominently in the chapters that follow. Christians believe that God created and is separate from the universe, for instance, and that human beings were made in God's image. These beliefs will be a central theme of chapter one. One of the most mysterious of Christian doctrines, the Trinity, will make an appearance in a passage on beauty in art in chapter two. But the distinguishing feature of Christianity has always been Christians' belief that Jesus was raised from the dead.

The second frequently mentioned perspective is materialism. By *materialism*, I mean the belief that the physical, material world is the ultimate reality—there is no supernatural God, gods or spirit(s). This view, or views somewhat like it, is sometimes referred to as naturalism or by still other names. I realize that when some readers hear the term *materialism*, their first thought has more to do Black Friday, outlet stores or the bumper sticker "He who dies with the most toys wins" than with a denial of the supernatural. Some people who are preoccupied with possessions also are materialists in the sense I have in mind here, but others are not; indeed, some of the best-known materialists, such as the Princeton ethicist Peter Singer, rail against the acquisitive tendencies of contemporary Westerners (including Christians who share this tendency). Despite the ambiguity of *materialism*, those who reject the existence of God or supernatural forces are usually described as materialists, and each of the alternative labels has flaws of its own. I will stick with the conventional terminology.

The best-known current materialists, New Atheists such as Richard Dawkins and Sam Harris, ground their materialism in evolutionary theory. They insist that human beings, together with all life on Earth, are the product of unguided Darwinian evolution. Although it is possible to be a materialist without also endorsing unguided evolution as the explanation for reality as we experience it, materialism and evolutionary theory are tightly linked in the contemporary world. Because of this, I will often focus on materialists who look to evolutionary explanations for the puzzles and paradoxes of our experience.

■ ■ ■

The introductory chapter of *True Paradox* lays the groundwork for my embrace of complexity by focusing first on two prominent and recent strategies for defending Christianity that implicitly reject the perspective I will be taking here. Each of the strategies is designed, or so it seems to me, to deny the complexity of the world as we actually experience it. The chapter also points out that Christians are not the only ones who seem to have trouble with complexity. Many of the best-known skeptics of Christianity flatten out complexity in a different way: by downplaying or even denying the intangible dimensions of human experience. They are a little like the triangles, squares and other shapes in the movie *Flatland*, who are comfortable in two dimensions but are disoriented by the evidence of a third.

The five chapters that follow consider a series of puzzles and paradoxes that each of us is familiar with—or at the least is likely to recognize once it is identified. I will begin with the puzzle of consciousness and the human obsession with devising elaborate ideas about the world and our place in it. After the mystery of ideas and idea making come chapters on beauty, suffering and sensation, justice, and finally life and afterlife.

My claim is a very simple one: Christianity tells us more about each of these paradoxes than you may think.

INTRODUCTION

Arguing About Origins

*Great Theater and a
Grand Distraction*

We all try to make sense of the universe. When Socrates said that the unexamined life isn't worth living, he may have been distinguishing those who are introspective and wrestle with moral questions from those who aren't and don't. But every one of us experiences a world of complexity, and we all try to piece our lives together in a way that gives them coherence and meaning. This is part of what it means to be human.

Although the complexity of our lives is not unique to our era, it has become more central to the human experience than ever before. A century ago, a grocery store might have offered one or two brands of cereal and, depending on where you were, possibly no olive oil at all. Today, a consumer has several dozen cereals to choose from, along with one or more varieties of virgin, extra virgin, fino and light olive oil. The psychologist Barry Schwartz tells us that the proliferation of choices makes consumers anxious.[1] We might be better off, he concludes, if we had fewer choices. But marketers do not seem to be heeding his cri de coeur.

We ourselves have created these consumer choices, as well as the ever-expanding array of new technology. But other elements of modern complexity were there all along; we just didn't know about them. Perhaps the most vivid illustration of these newly discovered complexities is Schrödinger's cat, a famous thought experiment proposed by a scientist named Erwin Schrödinger to Albert Einstein in 1935. Schrödinger asked Einstein to imagine putting a cat in a sealed box, along with a flask of poison that would be shattered, releasing the poison and killing the cat if a Geiger counter in the box detected radiation.

The radioactive decay that would enable a Geiger counter to detect radiation is both unpredictable and indeterminate in the short run. Because a tiny amount of radioactive material placed in the Geiger counter may or may not decay during the first hour of the experiment, the standard understanding of subatomic particles suggests that the cat would be both dead and alive during that period. In another experiment, less alarming to animal lovers, a scientist showed that an electron could be either a particle or a wave, depending on whether its movements were observed.

Any religion or system of thought that purports to be true needs to make sense of a world that is filled with these and other complexities. It may not have answers for every possible question now. After all, human understanding is sufficiently limited that some philosophers suspect there are some things we will never fully understand, such as the nature of human consciousness (our subject in chapter 1). But the capacity to provide explanations for some of the complexities of life as we actually experience it is a key test of any religion or system of thought that claims to offer a comprehensive account of our place in the universe.

In the past generation, materialist explanations of the universe have become more sophisticated than ever before. So too have strategies for defending Christianity. But the best-known—and seemingly successful—Christian and materialist accounts do quite poorly on the test I have just described. Although they are radically different in other respects, each has an odd tendency to deny some of the most important complexities of the world as we actually experience it. They are a little like politicians who answer the question they want to answer, rather than the question that was actually asked.

In the discussion that follows, I will focus first on two prominent strategies in the Christian apologetics of the past generation and then on the best-known materialist alternative. In each case, I will highlight the ways in which they sidestep complexity. I also will try to explain why this might be so.

The Limits of Simple Logic

A recent debate in a packed auditorium at North Carolina State University pitted a leading Christian apologist against an equally prominent atheist scientist. Their task: to convince the audience that there is, in the case of the apologist, or is not, for the atheist, "evidence to prove the existence of God."[2] No doubt inspired by *American Idol*, the format managed to combine two great Western institutions—courtroom arguments and a democratic vote—into a single evening's entertainment. After listening to opening statements, rebuttals and closing statements, the audience members weighed the evidence and then voted by secret ballot.

By all accounts, the evening was a success. The Christian apologist insisted that the universe had a beginning and that many signs point toward its creator being God; the scientist countered that the universe may simply be the one (if there is indeed just one) of an infinite number of universes that happens to support human life.

What interests me here is how the Christian apologist, a philosopher who teaches at a Christian college, outlined his case. The evidence for God, he argued, can be put "in the form of a deductive argument" consisting of four simple steps:

1. Everything that exists has an explanation of its existence (either in its own nature or in an external cause).

2. The universe exists.

3. If the universe has an explanation of its existence, that explanation is God.

4. Therefore, the explanation of the universe is God.

The Christian apologist insisted, in other words, that we can demonstrate God's existence as a matter of basic logic. This particular syllogism is derived from one of the most famous philosophical arguments for the existence of God, often known as the argument from first cause. If one thing or event causes another, the reasoning goes, there must be a first cause that set the whole train of events in motion; the most logical first cause is God.

Reasoning of this type, which is sometimes called natural theology, figured prominently in the writings of many of the great pagan and Christian thinkers of the early centuries. For the argument from first cause, we can thank Aristotle and later Thomas Aquinas. Another of the classic arguments is often associated with the great medieval theologian Anselm. Anselm contended that because God is the greatest being we can imagine, God must exist, a view known as the ontological argument. In each case, the proponent starts with premises that are sufficiently logical that they should be accepted by everyone and then attempts to construct arguments that will convince any rational person that God does indeed exist.

This mode of argument has become more popular than ever among Christianity's defenders in the past generation. Although the apologist in this particular debate is a superb debater—so much so that a prominent New Atheist called him "the one Christian apologist who seems to have put the fear of God into many of my fellow atheists"[3]—the embrace of logical proofs is, especially in less sophisticated hands, often a counterproductive strategy for showing that Christianity or some other system of thought is true. Before I explain why, I should provide a little more support for the claim that Christian apologetics has indeed taken the kind of philosophical turn I have just described. I can imagine several objections to my claim, even as it relates to the "evidence for God" debate. I'll focus on two.

Objection #1. The use of logic is unavoidable because the apologist is a philosopher; logic is his language. Of course, a Christian philosopher will use philosophy in his arguments, the reasoning might go, just as a law professor will invariably talk about law (just wait!). And a literature professor like C. S. Lewis, the Oxford don whose 1952 book *Mere Christianity* is the best-selling defense of Christianity of all time, will leaven his writings with references to novels and poems. We wouldn't expect him to do otherwise.

But this misses the point. If American Christians were not so enamored of these kinds of arguments, philosophy teachers probably would not be the ones going toe to toe with skeptics so often. It is interesting that we do not see more English professors or artists or poets on the frontline of these debates. Perhaps we should. After all, Christians believe we are part of a story in which God became one of us and lived among us, so perhaps artists and poets have something to say that would illuminate the story of our lives and the grand, beautiful narrative of Christianity. To be sure, some artists might be more inclined to let their work speak for itself, rather than mixing it up in the way philosophers routinely do. But many artists speak eloquently about their work, and art and literary critics participate in the same kinds of public events as philosophers. Yet they are rarely the ones who take center stage as defenders of Christianity.

Objection #2. I have overemphasized the Christian apologist's use of logic; it actually was only one tool in his arsenal. The apologist spent much of his allotted time arguing about the creation of the universe and the unlikelihood that its exquisite fine-tuning for life could have come about as the result of chance. Wasn't the syllogism simply a nifty rhetorical trick, this objection might conclude, a framework for the more elaborate arguments about the nature of the universe that followed? In some respects, it no doubt was. But abstract, philosophically tinged logic is ubiquitous in

recent arguments about Christianity, God and Christian morals—
so much so that *Christianity Today*, a bellwether Christian mag-
azine, devoted a cover story to Christian philosophers who have
revitalized the ancient tradition.[4]

The problem with these arguments—at least outside the context
of a structured debate—is that the philosophical turn has come a
generation too late. Fifty years ago, arguments relying on straightforward logic had more bite because basic premises about right and
wrong, and about what is or is not a good life, were widely shared.
Had today's Christian logicians appeared then, they might well
have found a receptive audience. But people no longer bring a
shared set of assumptions to these conversations. The irony is that
Christian apologetics began to embrace philosophy just as the
former consensus had begun to crumble.

In a world characterized by multiple sets of values and no single,
agreed-upon method of resolving differences, most of us simply
reject logical proofs of conclusions that conflict with our intuitions.
Presented with a syllogism that demonstrates the existence of God,
for instance, religious skeptics don't accept or even consider accepting the conclusion; they assume that one or more of the com-
ponent parts of the syllogism must be wrong. Take the Christian
apologist's four-part syllogism that (1) everything that exists has
an explanation of its existence; (2) the universe exists; (3) if the
universe has an explanation of its existence, that explanation is
God; and (4) therefore the explanation of the universe is God.

Looking at this syllogism, a skeptic might simply reject the third
step in the analysis. There may be other explanations for the universe than God, the skeptic might conclude—certainly Stephen

Hawking and other physicists seem to think so—which suggests that the syllogism must be flawed. Even generally sympathetic readers may have their doubts. When I showed an initial draft of this introduction to a friend who's an editor at a leading university press, she complained that the third step of the syllogism is "much more deeply unsettling than you or he say. . . . Calling the First Cause by that familiar name [God] seems to pile onto the First Cause all the familiar characteristics that we ascribe to our Judeo-Christian God, but none of them have any necessary connection with starting the universe." Still others might object to the apologist's first premise, asking why there must be an explanation for everything that exists.

I do not mean to suggest that philosophy has no value. My own son might disown me if I did, since he is well on his way to a philosophy degree and perhaps graduate work in philosophy. The tools of philosophy—such as a careful definition of terms and the use of sometimes fanciful hypotheticals (not so different from Schrödinger's cat) to tease out real-world implications—are extraordinarily useful and will figure at various points in my own analysis. The Socratic method, which is the standard technique in my own profession of teaching law, has a philosophical pedigree.

Nor do I mean to impugn the defenders of Christianity who use these techniques, least of all the extraordinarily talented apologist in the debate I described. The Christian philosophers of the past generation have achieved notable successes, perhaps the most important of which has been to undermine the secular consensus that theistic arguments have been debunked.[5] My point here is simply that readers who are not themselves Christian are not likely to be convinced by proofs based on simple logic, any more than Christians would be convinced by a simple logical argument that there is no God.

There is another very serious danger as well. Because those who hear these simple logical arguments are well aware that reality is highly complex, they may suspect that the arguments are not being made in good faith—that the defender of Christianity is trying to pull the wool over their eyes. The perception that defenders of Christianity may not be interested in truth and that they are not arguing in good faith is even more of an issue with the second popular strategy for defending Christianity. This strategy takes us from the world of philosophy to the world of law.

Losing the Truth in Court

In a recent post on a police officers' blog, a former prosecutor reminded his readers that "a trial is not about the truth." As evidence, he quoted a website that instructs criminal defense lawyers to make sure the jury instructions in their case "assure [*sic*] the jurors understand that . . . the question in a criminal case is not whether the defendant committed the acts of which he is accused," and that the instructions "avoid language that perpetuates the juror's intuitive inclination to make the trial a search for the truth."[6] The issue, instead, is whether prosecutors have demonstrated the defendant's guilt beyond a reasonable doubt. Alan Dershowitz, a Harvard law professor and occasional lawyer for celebrity defendants, has made much the same point:

> Even if it is "likely" or "probable" that this defendant committed the murder, he must be acquitted, because neither "likely" nor "probable" satisfies the daunting standard of proof

beyond a reasonable doubt. Accordingly, a legally proper result—acquittal in such a case—may not be the same as a morally just result. In such a case, justice has not been done to the victim, but the law has prevailed.[7]

In the column just quoted, Dershowitz was commenting on a jury's acquittal of a Florida woman who was accused of killing her two-year-old daughter. More recently, the acquittal in Florida of George Zimmerman for killing Trayvon Martin prompted President Obama to muse aloud that Martin reminded him of himself at a similar age. By the time you read these words, there probably will be another, equally surprising, headline-grabbing verdict in a criminal trial. However successful they may be in accomplishing other objectives, such as discouraging police officers from cutting corners when they gather evidence and ensuring that innocent defendants are rarely if ever sent to jail, American criminal trials are not a trustworthy guide to truth. Truth is not their objective.

Yet in the past generation, Christians—American Christians especially—have acted as if it is. Christian apologetics has relied on lawyers' arguments and the techniques of a criminal trial to defend the truth of Christianity, especially in debates over scientific evidence that seems to call the literal account of creation in the opening chapters of the Bible into question. Defenders of Christianity poke holes in the fossil record and trumpet disputes among scientists about the nature of evolution. In effect, the defenders of Christians have said, "If it doesn't fit, you must acquit."

Christianity on Trial

The pioneer of the current strategy was a law professor named

Phillip Johnson from the University of California–Berkeley. After decades of penning scholarly articles on criminal law and legal ethics, Johnson published a book called *Darwin on Trial* in 1991. As the title suggests, he proposed to put evolutionary theory "on trial," and in doing so to defend Christianity. His techniques were so popular that they have become ubiquitous, especially in debates on science and religion.

"What first drew my attention to the [science-religion debate]," Johnson writes at the outset of the book,

> was the way the rules of argument seemed to be structured to make it impossible to question whether what we are being told about evolution is really true. For example, the [scientific community's] rule against negative argument [that is, the stricture that only empirically testable propositions count as "science" and that arguments about the absence of evidence do not qualify] eliminates the possibility that science has not discovered how complex organisms could have developed. However wrong the current answer may be, it stands until a better answer arrives. *It is as if a criminal defendant were not allowed to present an alibi unless he could also show who did commit the crime.*[8]

The main chapters of the book subject various aspects of current evolutionary theory to stringent scrutiny. In one chapter Johnson contends that the fossil record is nearly as thin and as confused as it was in Darwin's era. Although evolutionary theorists point to molecular similarities such as the 99 percent congruence between human DNA and that of other species as evidence of evolution, species are separated by sharp distinctions, he argues in another. Johnson's skeptical survey of current evolutionary science in *Darwin on Trial* sparked the intelligent design movement, which does not reject evolution altogether, but contends that some characteristics of living organisms cannot be explained by evolutionary processes. The *mode* of Johnson's argument has been at least as influential as its content. It is the mode of argument that concerns me here.

As his title suggests, Johnson purports to expose Darwinism's flaws and inconsistencies by putting it on trial. But the real defendant for Johnson and the many apologists who have followed his precedent is Christianity. Christianity is the "criminal defendant" that is "not allowed to present an alibi" in the passage quoted above, and Darwinism is a witness against Christianity in the trial. *Cross-Examining Darwinism* might have been a more accurate title for the book.

Johnson was not the first to refer to trials and legal terminology in a defense of Christianity. The rhetoric of law has been popular for some time. But there is an important difference between Johnson and his predecessors. Whereas other defenders of Christianity interviewed Christian experts and assembled evidence—in books with titles like *Evidence That Demands a Verdict* and *The Case for Christ*[9]—Johnson actually used the legal techniques he described. He vigorously cross-examined the implied Darwinian "witness" against Christianity, just as a defense lawyer confronting the prosecution's star witness might do. As with simple logical arguments in defense of Christianity, this strategy is often effective but it carries very high costs.

A criminal defense lawyer who is cross-examining a witness for the prosecution often tries to *prevent* the witness from telling her story. "Some witnesses come to court eager to tell all they know and to expound their ideas to the fullest extent at every opportunity," one cross-examination manual says. "If the cross-examiner fails to stop the rambling, the witness may disclose prejudicial material or even take the testimony into areas where the cross-examiner is unprepared."[10] "A lawyer does not win by asking the most questions on cross-examination," according to another expert. "Rather, a lawyer wins by getting the answers needed to advance his case or to weaken the adversary's case."[11] Criminal lawyers also fight hard to make sure that the jury never sees evidence that suggests the defendant may actually have committed the crime. If the police have discovered a possible murder weapon, you can be sure that the defense lawyer will insist that it was improperly obtained—perhaps through an illegal search—and that it should be disallowed.

These techniques make sense for a criminal trial—since we want to make sure that innocent defendants are not convicted and put in jail—but they are a deeply problematic way to show the truth of Christianity. If we view Christianity as the defendant in a criminal trial, we no longer will simply follow the evidence wherever it leads. We will pursue the trails that lead to Christianity while trying to deflect attention from the ones that seem to call Christianity into doubt. Our objective is mounting a lawyer's case: discredit the findings of evolutionary theory here, call the personal integrity of Darwin's defenders into question there. This is standard practice for defense attorneys in a criminal trial. Indeed, most defense attorneys carefully avoid asking their client if he actually committed the offense; the lawyer fears that knowing the truth might interfere with his defense.

To put it plainly, truth is not the principal objective of a criminal trial. This is why Americans do not assume that acquittal in a criminal trial proves that the defendant is innocent. As tempting as it is to borrow the techniques of criminal defense lawyers, they are a poor strategy for showing that Christianity or any other set of beliefs is true.

Logical defenses of Christianity and deft lawyerly parries are problematic for another reason as well. They are distractions. Each of these techniques tends to emphasize *how* God created the heavens, the earth, and us, rather than what the creation is like. The reluctance to wrestle with the complexity of the world as we actually experience it is understandable, but it is this world that any religion or other system of thought needs to explain if it purports to be true.

Materialists' Discomfort with the Intangible

While Christianity's defenders have embraced a pair of problematic techniques, religious skeptics seem to me to have made two very large errors of their own. First, the best-known materialists, including both the New Atheists and less polemical advocates of similar views, insist on counting as evidence only that which is measurable and quantifiable. The model that drives their thinking is the scientific method, in which a hypothesis is subject to repeated and repeatable experimental tests. Even the more extreme of these materialists, such as Richard Dawkins, acknowledge that we need other sources of knowledge, such as history and sociology, to determine, for example, the date on which Caesar crossed the Rubicon or what conditions were like in field hospitals in the Civil War. Yet they often treat intangible factors and the disciplines and perspectives that emphasize them as irrelevant or suspect. Scientism, as a materialist critic of this perspective puts it, "easily generates a conviction that other forms of inquiry simply do not measure up."[12]

But discounting the less tangible features of our experience rules out some of the most important evidence about the nature of reality. Human beings sense many things that cannot be seen, touched or quantified. Sensations like longing or horror, outrage or love seem real to those who feel them, and nearly everyone feels them to some degree. What do they represent? Where do they come from? On these questions, the best-known materialists are notably weak. Even the subtlest of the leading lights, such as psychologist and linguist Steven Pinker, rely on highly speculative claims about the nature of human consciousness.

In a magisterial work on the decline of violence, Pinker seems at times to distill consciousness to reason, empathy and a cluster of primitive emotions (such as vengefulness) that are best suppressed. "Most applications of the moral sense," he writes, "are not particularly moral but rather tribal, authoritarian, or puritanical, and it is reason that tells us which of the other applications we should entrench as norms."[13] Love and longing seem to fall out of the picture altogether, except as a lubricant for reproduction.

The skeptics' second mistake is to ignore the deeply puzzling nature of human morality and law. It is not especially surprising that all of us—unless we are being willfully perverse—believe in moral codes. Although most deny any universal basis for morality, materialists do propound codes of morality. Princeton ethicist Peter Singer has passionately defended a moral code that calls on the wealthy to contribute large portions of their income to those who are less well off.[14] Richard Dawkins has outlined ten commandments for an atheist to live by.[15] Even a person who is convinced that the universe is heartless—that the cosmos is all there is—may believe in making it a little less heartless by his or her life.

None of this is news. The real puzzle is that our moral codes hold human beings to standards of honesty and selflessness that none of us can meet. To make matters worse, the systems of law we construct to enforce these standards don't work. They can't manage to steer human behavior in the directions lawmakers and law enforcers desire. Why do we human beings think we can establish a just social order even after an endless succession of failed attempts to do so? Because religious skeptics sharply limit the evidence they are willing to consider, turning the conversation to issues that can be tested with the tools of current science, they have very little to say about this enduring puzzle of human morality.

Because the defenders of Christianity have been preoccupied with simple logical arguments and lawyerly techniques, they too have neglected this puzzle. The debate centers on how we or the universe were created. Neither side has a great deal to say about life as we actually experience it.

Cosmology Is Not Enough

When I outline these concerns in talks to Christian audiences, someone nearly always complains that I am asking the defenders of Christianity to lay down their arms just as we are about to win a key battle. The battle is over the origins of the universe; the victory is a triumph in the debate. And the battle seems to be going quite well for Christians.

A century ago, many religious skeptics insisted that the universe was not created; it simply existed and continues to exist. Although Albert Einstein believed in the existence of a higher power, he assumed that the universe must be static when he devised his theory of relativity. Because the theory implied that the universe was either expanding or contracting, he added a "cosmological constant" to compensate for the unacceptable gyrations. (To his credit, Einstein later acknowledged this adjustment to be one of his greatest blunders.) In a 1948 debate with Jesuit priest and philosopher Frederick Copleston, Bertrand Russell, the philosopher and leading popular atheist of the early and mid-twentieth century, rejected the Christian teaching that the universe was created by God. "I should say that the universe is just there," he insisted, and "that's all."[16]

A growing body of evidence suggests that Russell got this particular issue wrong and that the universe did have a beginning, as Christian (and some other religions') accounts of God creating the heavens and the earth suggest. The first major hint of what scientists now call the Big Bang came in 1929, when Edwin Hubble determined through observation that the universe does seem to be expanding. Subsequent measurements have provided considerably more confirming evidence. Most recently, scientists found evidence of the Higgs boson, which is implied in the mathematics of the Big Bang, through an astonishing sequence of experiments conducted in the Large Hadron Collider, a circular reactor outside

Geneva that is nearly twenty miles in circumference.

Still, some physicists who reject Christianity argue that our universe could, in effect, have created itself and that the tiny probability that our universe would have features that allowed for the emergence of life may be less remarkable if our universe is simply one of an enormous number of universes. In the afterword of a book by a prominent physicist (the same one who defended atheism in the North Carolina State debate) who purports to show how a universe could emerge from "nothing," Richard Dawkins gushes that "even the last remaining trump card of the theologian, 'Why is there something rather than nothing?,' shrivels up before your very eyes."[17]

Defenders of Christianity are understandably eager to counter these claims. But winning this ongoing battle over origins is not the same as winning the war, in this case over the truth or falsity of Christian beliefs.

Changing the Subject

I do not mean to suggest that the defenders of Christianity should simply bow out of these debates. But Christianity's defenders need to recognize that cosmology alone is not enough to show the truth of Christianity or any other system of thought. If a system of thought is true, it must also explain the character of creation— what it is like.

If we shift from origins to the world as we actually experience it, we will need to explain sensations like our sense of beauty and evil, as well as the puzzles of morals and law. An ancient religion like Christianity may seem ill-equipped to make sense of these puzzles, every one of which is paradoxical in key respects. But precisely the opposite is true. We will find, I think, that Christianity is considerably more plausible (and materialism and other systems of thought somewhat less) than you may think.

The place to begin is with human consciousness. Here, too, it would be easy to devote all our attention to the question of where human consciousness came from—the question of whether unguided evolution can explain consciousness or whether only God could have created it. If we wish to expand the inquiry, we will need to avoid this temptation and go straight to the more central issue of what consciousness is like.

1

IDEAS AND IDEA MAKING

Consciousness, which the *American Heritage Dictionary* defines as the "critical awareness of one's own identity and situation," is the single most complex and mysterious feature of our existence. Consciousness is the subjectivity of our experience—what it feels like to be human. Our sense of self and our ability to reflect on our past or make plans for the future are all elements of our consciousness. Even if we could trace every connection among the estimated one hundred billion neurons in our brains, our sense of self would transcend the picture provided by this physical map.[1] It is somehow more than the sum of our parts. If there is a "ghost in the machine," as philosophers used to imagine, consciousness is that awe-inspiring ghost.

"The existence of consciousness is both one of the most familiar and one of the most astounding things about the world," the philosopher Thomas Nagel (a religious skeptic) has written. "No conception of the natural order that does not reveal it as something to be expected can aspire even to the outline of completeness."[2]

The most remarkable dimension of human consciousness is our capacity for abstract thought, including our ability to develop or debate theories of reality such as the perspectives we are considering in this book: philosophical accounts of our origins, Marxist theories of history, scientific explanations that deny the existence of God, religious explanations that proclaim it. Rather than using an unlovely and less precise term such as *reason* or *cognition*, I will call the ability to devise and assess theories about the nature of reality our *idea-making capacity*.

Although we tend to take our idea-making capacity for granted, it actually is quite peculiar. From an early age, most of us puzzle over the mysteries of politics, economics, and personal and social ethics. We have not only the capacity to formulate and debate ideas about morality and other features of our existence and to adopt theories about why we are here and how we should live, but also a veritable compulsion to do so. Why in the world do we do this? What purpose does our idea making serve? After all, it is not immediately clear why it is necessary to our survival as individuals or as a species.

It is possible, of course, that our idea-making capacity is simply a game and that our theories about how to live may stretch our minds yet have no greater significance. It also is possible that our preoccupation with abstract theories about reality is an accidental byproduct of other, more meaningful, human traits. But it is highly unlikely that a capacity that is so central to our experience is, in a sense, a mistake—that it has no purpose. If a religion or system of thought is true, it should give us insight into what that purpose is.

In addition to explaining why idea making matters, the other key test for a religion or system of thought is the *content* of the ideals it advocates. Every religion and system of thought gives rise to its own distinctive morality and norms of behavior. If a religion or system of thought is true, its ideals should be true for every culture, not just for the culture in which they emerged. Ideals that make sense only in ancient Palestine, eighth-century Arabia or the twentieth-first century West cannot plausibly claim to be transcendent truth. They need to make sense in all places and times.

Our idea-making capacity is the most mystifying dimension of our experience, and it is possible that we will never fully understand it. But we can learn a great deal about the plausibility of a religion or system of thought from its insights into the purpose of idea making and from the content of its moral ideals.

What Is the Purpose of Our Idea-Making Capacity?

Given that contemporary materialism is so closely allied with evolutionary theory (in practice, that is—the two need not go together), deciphering the purpose of idea making would seem to be a strong suit for materialists, and perhaps more problematic for Christianity, Judaism and other religions. Many contemporary materialists revel in their ability to unravel mysteries of adaptation. When advocates of intelligent design insisted that the compound eye, with its highly complex structure, could not be the product of evolution, evolutionary theorists (most of whom, but certainly not all, are materialists) responded with intriguingly plausible accounts of the adaptive benefits that may have come from intermediate steps on the path to a compound eye. Sensitivity to light may confer an advantage, for instance, even if it does not enable the organism to see as sight is ordinarily understood.

Yet materialists have much less to say about the mysteries of human consciousness. Some materialists suggest that our idea-making capacity doesn't have a purpose at all—or at least that our mental capacities have far outstripped the most important benefits. Some features of the outsized human brain were essential to early survival. Our facility with language, for instance, enabled us to coordinate and plan. But the species would have done just fine, these materialists suggest, if we never had developed the capacity to devise and debate elaborate systems of morality.

Steven Pinker sums up nicely the notion that our idea-making capacity may be extraneous. It is true, he acknowledges, that people in every place and time "concoct theories of the universe and their place within it." But to his mind, this yearning is "biologically frivolous and vain."[3] He explains that "given that the mind is a product of natural selection, it should not have a miraculous ability to commune with all truths; it should have a mere ability to solve problems that are sufficiently similar to the mundane survival challenges of our ancestors." From this perspective, religion, philosophy and the quest to make sense of why we are here are "the application of mental tools to problems they were not designed to solve."[4]

Call this the runaway evolution explanation. Many evolutionary theorists' favorite illustration of this phenomenon, dating back to Darwin himself, is the peacock's tail. They speculate that the beautiful colors of a male peacock's tail evolved to signal a male's desirability as a mate. Although the signal was adaptive, it led to an evolutionary arms race, with peacocks' tails getting ever larger and more ostentatious, to the point where they interfered with survival;

it isn't easy for a bird with an outsized tail to get airborne to evade predators. The materialists who explain our idea-making capacity as an unnecessary byproduct of the expansion of the human brain are in a sense suggesting that this is another context in which an evolutionary process overshot the mark.

Other materialists attribute some adaptive significance to the most pervasive form of idea making, religion, including Pinker in other articles and books. But even the most nuanced of these accounts gives short shrift to the complexity and richness of religion. According to the standard account in evolutionary psychology, the widespread belief in a supernatural being or beings, which appears to date back to the earliest humans, is best explained by a phenomenon known as "hypersensitive agency detection."[5] Like other animals, the reasoning goes, we developed an acute sense of possible predators. Humans who imagined that every rustling in the tall grass of the African savannah was a lion were more likely to survive than their peers who assumed that the rustling was simply the wind. False positives (mistakenly thinking a predator was nearby even when it wasn't) are better than false negatives (thinking the sound is not a predator when it is)—at least so long as they did not leave our ancestors so paralyzed by fear that they couldn't function.

According to this view, the tendency to imagine that a living being lay behind every sight and sound on the landscape caused humans to detect living agents everywhere, even in the sky. "Suppose," as the psychologist Jonathan Haidt puts it, early humans "begin attributing agency to the weather. (Thunder and lightning sure make it *seem* as though somebody up in the sky is angry at us.)

Suppose a group of humans begins jointly creating a pantheon of invisible agents who cause the weather, and other assorted cases of good or bad fortune. Voila—the birth of supernatural agents."[6]

The first thing to note is that the step from hearing a rustle in the tall grass and suspecting a lion to a conclusion that the entire cosmos has been ordered by God is not a small one. It is better described as an Olympian leap. The usefulness of heightened sensitivity to the possible presence of lions is far more obvious than, for instance, the benefits of detecting gods in or behind the cosmos. Some of the more recent accounts attempt to address this shortcoming, positing that the earliest religious beliefs were an accident of our hypersensitive agency, but that religion proved to be an effective means of enhancing the cohesiveness of a particular group.[7] Religion was an accident, the reasoning goes, but it proved to be a happy accident (at least in this sense).

I do not mean to suggest that these accounts are entirely misguided. It is possible that there are elements of truth to them. It certainly is the case that vibrant religious communities experience high levels of social cohesion, for instance, and this no doubt is one reason for the emergence and spread of religion. But even the most sophisticated materialist accounts of religion leave out its most important dimension: we are drawn to a particular religion or philosophy because it seems to us to better explain the nature of the universe than the alternatives. This feature is central to our embrace of a particular religion or system of thought, or so it has seemed to men and women in all places and times. Yet it seems to be left on the cutting-room floor in the materialist accounts of religion.

It is useful to compare materialism to the gods and goddesses of Greek mythology in this regard. No one takes Greek mythology seriously as a theory of reality now, because its explanations of the universe no longer seem plausible. Materialism obviously explains far more of the world than Greek mythology does. But Greek mythology fares surprisingly well on the particular issue we are considering here: the purpose of our idea-making capacity.

The Greeks believed that the gods and goddesses were capricious, sometimes responding with loyalty and love, but also prone to jealousy, anger and infidelity. Hera's displeasure at Paris's conclusion that Aphrodite was the most beautiful of the three leading goddesses ultimately led, as Homer has it in *The Iliad*, to the awful carnage of the Trojan War. Knowing how to appease the gods required all of a person's critical wits, as well as the assistance of specialists such as the diviners who interpreted the entrails of animals that had been sacrificed or the meaning of the sudden appearance of a hawk in the sky. It is not hard to see how our idea-making capacity would be useful in a world of Greek gods and goddesses.

Other religions—from Hinduism to Christianity to New Age spiritualism—also seem to me to more fully explain the usefulness of our idea-making capacity than materialism does. Let me emphasize once again that we cannot rule out the possibility that this key feature of human consciousness is indeed an accidental byproduct—that it is our peacock's tail. But it does not seem likely that our hands, feet, liver and heart are useful adaptations yet our idea-making capacity was an accident.

Moreover, even if our idea-making capacity were the byproduct of other traits, this still does not explain why idea making is so central to our sense of what it means to be human. There is something deeply unsatisfying about the claim that idea making has no real meaning.

Perhaps you find the materialist account persuasive. You are in very good company if you do. But I hope you will agree that the mismatch between the limited role that idea making plays in the materialist account and its central importance to our sense of what it means to be human should, at the very least, give us pause.

The Unreasonable Usefulness of Mathematics

Christianity offers a very different explanation of our idea-making capacity. Christians believe that the heavens reflect the glory of God (in the words of Psalm 19) and that humans are made in God's image (Genesis 1:26-27). These beliefs imply that the universe is rational and intelligible, since it reflects the glory of a personal, intelligent creator; and that our idea-making capacity will help us to better function in the universe, since we are made in the image of its creator. Ironically, given the perceived frictions between religion and science, the Christian belief in the intelligibility of the universe propelled the emergence of modern science. The conviction that the universe is the rational creation of a rational God was what got Isaac Newton out of bed in the morning. And the same was true of many other giants of the scientific revolution.

One remarkable piece of evidence in support of the Christian belief—which is shared with Judaism and Islam—that our idea-making capacity is not accidental comes from the history of abstract math and a famous article called "The Unreasonable Effectiveness of Mathematics in the Natural Sciences." When mathematicians theorized about complex numbers (numbers that consist of a real number together with the square root of a negative one), they were working with a purely invented concept.

The article's author writes, "Most more advanced mathematical concepts, such as complex numbers, algebras, linear operators, Borel sets . . . were so devised that they are apt subjects on which the mathematician can demonstrate his ingenuity and sense of formal beauty."[8] They might easily have been dismissed as intricate, complex and of no obvious use for human survival and flourishing. Yet complex numbers have subsequently proven indispensable to our understanding of quantum mechanics—the principles governing subatomic particles. This sequence has been repeated sufficiently often that it cannot easily be dismissed as the product of chance. Using their idea-making capacity at its most abstract, men and women devise and discover concepts that later prove to be enormously useful. The seemingly irrelevant has transformative significance.

To be sure, the "unreasonable effectiveness of mathematics" is not ubiquitous. For every abstract innovation that later helps us to better understand the universe, there are many that do not prove so useful. But this is to be expected. Even if we are made in the image of the rational, intelligent creator of the universe, there would be no reason to expect that every abstract thought produced by the most brilliant among us would expand our understanding of the universe. But the fact that some of the most beautiful products (indeed, it is often the most beautiful products) of our idea-making capacity are so useful is almost miraculous. "Something has happened," as Thomas Nagel puts it, "that has gotten our minds into immediate contact with the rational order of the world."[9]

From a materialist perspective, the unreasonable effectiveness of mathematics is very difficult to explain. It is as if we somehow happened to hit the cosmic jackpot. There is, after all, no need to understand complex numbers on the African savannah and thus no reason to suspect from a purely evolutionary perspective that our rational speculations would give us insights into the nature of the universe. Yet somehow they do. There is no reason to expect that the universe is intelligible. Yet it is. The usefulness of mathematics is equally inexplicable for adherents of pantheistic religions, who believe that gods inhere in the operations of nature, since these perspectives do not offer any reason to expect there to be a rational order to the universe. For Christianity and the other monotheistic religions, by contrast, math's unreasonable effectiveness is perfectly natural. It is what we would expect.

The Personal Usefulness of Our Idea-Making Capacity

If our idea-making capacity genuinely matters, its usefulness should be reflected in a very different way as well: a religion or system of thought that is a plausible candidate for truth should make us better able to handle the circumstances of our lives. The suggestion that personal accounts of how a set of ideas has transformed a person's life are evidence that the ideas may be true, and that the absence of such testimonials is reason to doubt the ideas, may seem odd. But if our idea-making capacity is central to our experience as human beings, the effect of a set of ideas on the lives of its adherents is a key test of its plausibility.

Testimonials—often referred to as a person's "testimony"—date back to the earliest years of Christianity. Both the term and its importance figured prominently in the trial of the apostle Paul, as recounted in the New Testament. After his arrest for allegedly disrupting the peace, Paul defended himself by telling the story of his conversion. He spoke first to the crowd around him at the time of his arrest, recounting how Jesus had appeared to him as he traveled to Damascus, saying, "Saul, Saul, why are you persecuting me?" an encounter that transformed every aspect of his life (including his name; he is identified as Paul, rather than Saul, from this point on).

Paul repeated the story during formal legal proceedings before the governor and king, telling them that Jesus appointed him as a servant and witness to the forgiveness of sins that Jesus offers; that he had proclaimed the promise of Jesus in Damascus, Jerusalem, Judea and in Gentile regions; and that "to this day I have had the help that comes from God, testifying both to small and great."[10]

Testimonies have been a central feature of Christianity ever since. The most famous testimony is Augustine's account of his conversion to Christianity in *The Confessions*, which was written in roughly A.D. 397–400. "Our heart is restless," he wrote in a meditation to God, "until it rests in you."[11] A prominent modern example was *Born Again*, a considerably less literary but highly influential testimony by convicted Watergate felon Charles Colson. In many Christian churches, new members are expected to describe—orally or in writing—how they came to accept the truth of Christianity and how it has changed their lives. Some may have been raised in Christian families, while others came to Christianity after years of drug abuse or alcoholism.

Stories about how a set of ideas has changed a person's life are not unique to Christianity. The question that the youngest child asks at a Jewish Passover dinner—"Why is this night different than any other night?"—is the preface to a collective testimony about God's deliverance of the Jews from Egypt and setting them apart as his chosen people. Other religions also have testimonies. One of my own favorites during my college years, before I first embraced Christianity, was a book called *Zen and the Art of Motorcycle Maintenance.*

To their credit, the New Atheists and other materialists have placed increasing emphasis on their own testimonials. In an advertising campaign a few years ago, a group of atheists posted signs on London buses, saying, "There's probably no god. Now stop worrying and enjoy your life." If the lives of materialists did improve after adopting a materialist perspective, this would indeed be relevant evidence of the truth of materialism. Richard Dawkins has devoted an entire book to commending the wonders of life as experienced from a materialist perspective. Aimed at adolescents, *The Magic of Reality* attempts to show how scientific inquiry has unlocked the logic of the seemingly miraculous—from rainbows to the origins of the universe—and to demonstrate that the discoveries of science offer as much wonder and life satisfaction as religious belief.[12]

Another prominent materialist scientist recently proclaimed that understanding our place in the web of being fills her life with joy. "I am proud to be part of the riot of nature," she wrote, "to know that the same forces that produced me also produced bees, giant ferns and microbes that live at the bottom of the sea."[13] These testimonies suggest that the popular atheists and other leading materialists recognize that personal testimonies are essential to a system of thought's plausibility. Only if the ideas improve the lives of adherents in discernible ways are they a credible candidate for truth.

Thus far, these materialist testimonies appear to be limited to a small number of well-educated materialists in developed countries. But recent studies do show that the number of "nones"—citizens who do not have any religious affiliation—has risen significantly in the United States and other Western countries. There is even a movement to start atheist churches to promote materialist values. "It's all the best bits of church, but with no religion and awesome pop songs," as one of the founders of Sunday Assembly put it.[14] If these developments were to produce compelling testimonials, the testimonials would add to the evidence for materialism; if not, they will have the opposite effect.

The Universality of Ideals

The other test of a religion or system of thought, in addition to its explanation of why idea making matters, is the content of its ideals. If a religion or system of thought is a plausible candidate for truth, it will give rise to moral ideals that hold true in every season—ideals that transcend time and place. Because cultural norms are constantly changing, the ideals will need to have seemingly contradictory characteristics. First, they should seem plausible at all times and places, whether in an ancient agrarian society or a modern industrial one.

But the ideas also must have critical bite—they must call conventional wisdom into question—in the same range of societies.

The most plausible religions or systems of thought include elements that seem unusual or even preposterous for the time in which the relevant system was generated, yet persuasive and true from our perspective. Likewise, they will include elements that run strongly counter to the conventional wisdom of our own place and time—not because they are rooted in another place and time but because our age, like all ages, has its own moral blind spots.

With this yardstick, we can quickly see why so many familiar systems of thought fall short. Although we rightly admire the democratic values of classical Greece, for instance, they are not a plausible candidate for universal truth. During the same period that saw the world's first democracy in Golden Age Athens, enlightened opinion considered women unqualified for citizenship. The same culture treated the exposure of unwanted children—that is, dumping them in the wilderness with the expectation they would die—as perfectly acceptable behavior, as did the Romans. Tacitus, the Roman historian, insisted that the Jews were "sinister and revolting" because they taught that it is a serious sin to kill an unwanted child.[15] One could put the classical ideals in a more attractive light, of course. But whatever light one uses, the ideals do not the stand the test of time. Although we marvel at some features of these ideals, no one would seriously claim they are universally true.

Even the Mosaic law—the original biblical law, set forth in the first five books of the Old Testament—falls short of these standards for universality. The Mosaic law was far superior to the ideals of surrounding societies in the ancient Near East. The Canaanite religions of the areas immediately outside ancient Israel practiced child sacrifice and cult prostitution. Both are condemned in the Mosaic law and other Old Testament writings (Deuter-onomy 12:31; Proverbs 23:27-28). Yet large swaths of the Mosaic law—such as its requirements that land be returned to its original owners at periodic intervals, that farmers leave the gleanings of their crops for the poor, that mildewed houses be quarantined—were clearly written with a particular time and place (and agricul-tural economy) in mind. These ideals do not translate readily to other times and places.

The materialist credos of our own day suffer from precisely the opposite problem: they fit a little too comfortably with the assump-tions of twenty-first-century Western elites. One recent list of ma-terialist "commandments" includes items such as "treat your fellow human beings, your fellow living things and the world in general with love, honesty, faithfulness and respect" and "never seek to censor or cut yourself off from dissent; always respect the rights of others to disagree with you."[16] Most materialists also reject tradi-tional sexual morality. There is nothing in the standard package of materialist beliefs that would puzzle or alarm the average reader of the *New York Review of Books*.

One obvious reason materialist ideals tend to fit so comfortably with the norms of contemporary elite culture is that materialism itself doesn't imply any particular set of ideals. Materialism cannot yet explain why ideas and idea making matter. The materialists' own creeds are thus add-ons—they do not come from materialism itself. This doesn't mean that materialists themselves take their ideals lightly; many materialists honor the values they espouse and live admirable lives. But because materialists are busy devising them now, their ideals tend to mirror the values of current elite

Western culture. There is little in them that seems unusual, much less preposterous, to the culture in which they have emerged.

To be sure, some materialists have taken provocative positions on particular ethical issues. Princeton professor Peter Singer contends that euthanasia of children who are mentally impaired is sometimes appropriate and argues that Westerners should contribute the vast majority of their wealth to efforts to relieve human suffering around the world. Yet Singer's views go well beyond the stance of most materialists. And even his views are extreme versions of commitments—to abortion in the first case and poverty relief in the second—that are widely held by *New York Review of Books* readers. This is a sign that the ideals are not likely to reflect universal truth.

At this point, an objection is no doubt welling up in many readers' throats: Isn't the standard I am holding these ideals up to impossible to meet? Could any set of ideals ever seem plausible both in ancient cultures and in modern ones, yet also have critical bite in the same cultures? The standard is indeed daunting, all but impossible. But Christianity does surprisingly well on the test I have been applying.

Christianity's most distinctive ideals are its insistence on loving even our enemies and its embrace of human equality. Christians believe each of us is made in the image of God. "There is neither Jew nor Greek," the Bible also says, "there is neither slave nor free, there is no male and female, for you are all one in Christ Jesus" (Galatians 3:28). In the contemporary West, we take the importance of equality for granted. The idea that men should not be favored over women or one ethnic group over another is common coinage. (I am talking about ideals now, not whether Christians or any existing society achieves them.)

But these values were not common coinage at all in the ancient Middle East. Rigid distinctions, not equality, were the norm in ancient Middle Eastern societies. Landowners were superior to those who worked the land, women had little standing, and slaves were expendable—they could be beaten or killed for little reason. When the Romans took control of Palestine, they introduced a more formal system of rights. But Rome had its own rigid distinctions differentiating among citizens, between free noncitizens and slaves, and between men and women.

Christianity's commitment to equality was astonishing. When Jesus told the parable of the good Samaritan—which praises the kind intervention of a Samaritan man to assist a Jew who had been beaten and robbed, at a time when Jesus' fellow Jews despised Samaritans—he called the legitimacy of traditional ethnic boundaries into question. Both the Old and the New Testament grant women a measure of dignity that was highly unusual for the time. Women figured quite prominently in the early church—as benefactors, leaders of house churches and in other capacities. Some scholars believe that Christianity's treatment of women was a key factor in its remarkable growth in the Roman Empire in the first few centuries of the Common Era. (The Roman Emperor Valentinian was sufficiently worried about Christianity's attractiveness to women that he issued an order in 370 forbidding Christian missionaries from making visits to the houses of pagan women.)[17] In each of these respects, the Christian ideal of equality seems remarkably modern.

Yet this Christian egalitarianism is not the blind, sappy kind that prevails in current Western thought. Equality in current thinking has an absolutist quality, denying that there are any relevant differences between us. This insistence that we all be treated as equal in every respect seems to be a legacy of eighteenth-century Enlightenment thinking. It is an attempt to ignore the inevitable differences we have—whether we are men or women, old or young, disabled or fully able—even if those differences are highly relevant for the task at hand. If you have ever wondered why a frail, middle-aged woman is as likely to be subjected to an extensive search at the airport as someone who is a far more plausible threat to security, our obsession with equality is the explanation. The typical scholarly article or public discussion of the US Constitution's Equal Protection Clause assumes that we are like so many billiard balls: different colors, perhaps, but all the same size and shape.

Christian equality rejects the view that we are interchangeable, insisting instead that each of us has a baseline dignity that comes from being made in our Creator's image. The principal metaphor for Christian equality is the body. As the Bible puts it, some of us are like hands, others like feet, still others the eyes or ears (1 Corinthians 12:12-20). Each of us has a valuable role, but our roles are different. Christianity refuses to pretend otherwise and is, in this sense, out of step with current sensibilities.

Equally offensive to modern Westerners, Christianity also embraces what, to us, seems an unduly strict code of sexual conduct. The secular understanding of Christian sexual ethics begins with the misperception (which unfortunately sometimes is also shared by Christians) that sex and the body are bad. The Bible teaches that a husband and wife become one flesh when they marry (Genesis

2:24)—a clear reference to sexual intercourse—and it contains pages of vivid and frank love poetry. Christianity leaves no doubt that sexuality and the body are good.

Yet Christianity also teaches that the precious gift of sex is intended only for marriage. Although confining sex to marriage may seem oppressive, there is at least some evidence that it makes for better marriages—and some would argue, better sex. A recent study shows, for instance, that men and women who have fewer sexual partners before marriage are more likely to be faithful to their spouse and less likely to divorce.[18]

The evidence about the benefits of the two-parent households in which this sex takes place is far stronger. Although it is trendy to extoll the benefits of nontraditional families, and modern reproductive technology has made it easier than ever for a single man or woman to have a child, children who are raised in families with two parents appear to do better by every yardstick, whether it is graduating from college, physical health, social problems or staying out of jail.[19] The results hold true even in countries like Sweden that provide extensive support for nontraditional families.[20]

Christian sexual ethics stand in tension with the Middle Eastern moral code for precisely the opposite reason. The same teachings that Westerners criticize as unduly restrictive are condemned in the Arab world as too lax. The Arab sexual code discourages casual interaction between men and women, not just sex. Jesus' encounters with women, which scandalized the conventions of first-century Palestine, would violate the sexual norms of many Arab countries today. He talked openly with a Samaritan woman he encountered at a public well, asking her for a drink of water; he welcomed Mary

Magdalene into his entourage; and his closest friends included two women named Mary and Martha. As exemplified by Jesus himself, Christianity not only permits casual interaction between the sexes; it teaches that segregation of the sexes is usually linked to a failure to recognize the dignity of women.

Christian understandings of egalitarianism and Christian sexual ethics are perhaps the most obvious components of Christian morality that deviate from modern Western norms. But they are not the only ones. Christianity embraces honor and courage to a degree that seems embarrassing to modern Westerners but seemed (and seems) admirable to people in most places and times, including the contemporary Middle East. The morality that comes from the Christian belief that God made humans in his image and made himself human looks funny to many today, and it looked funny to many in the ancient world. But it looks funny for different reasons. None of this proves that Christianity is true, but it is evidence (counterintuitive evidence, to be sure) that Christianity is more plausible than many people think.

Why Are Christians So Bad?

Some may reply that Christians themselves are equally powerful evidence that Christian ideals should be rejected rather than embraced. This objection takes two different forms. The first version focuses on how modern Christians behave. If we look at current divorce rates, we see they are just as high among Christians in some areas as they are among other Americans. Christians also can be found indulging in some of the same sexual adventures as other Americans. The owner of a strip club in Tampa told a *New York*

Times reporter that his business thrived during an event held by Promise Keepers—an organization that calls men to recommit to biblical values, especially in their marriages.[21] Many of the men who came to the strip club did not even take off the name badges they wore to the conference.

This objection is similar to the puzzle of Christians who do not seem to act any better than those who reject Christianity. It speaks poorly of Christians, but it is important to keep in mind that Christians who take advantage of easy divorce laws and easy access to nonmarital sex are violating Christian morality, not upholding it. Christianity teaches that sin is inevitable and that Jesus became human so that our sins might be forgiven. But it also instructs Christians to honor marriage and to avoid even looking at someone other than their spouse with lustful intent.

The second version of this objection is concerned with what Christians say—that is, with the values they identify with Christianity. The issue here is not abortion or same-sex marriage or any of the social issues we struggle with today (although I believe they have been affected). The most egregious example is American slavery. In the best account of this sad history, *America's God*, Mark Noll shows that proslavery advocates often put abolitionists on the defensive by pointing out that the Old Testament patriarchs had slaves and the New Testament never explicitly instructs slave holders to release their slaves. "Let [the president of Wheaton College] shew from the Bible," as one proslavery advocate put it, "that the Patriarchs did not hold slaves: let him prove from that authority, that . . . the Apostles excluded slave-holders from the church of God."[22]

Although Christian abolitionists made rejoinders that should have been compelling—the Bible at best tolerates slavery as a ubiquitous feature of the ancient Roman economy; neither the Romans nor the Bible ever endorsed the kidnapping of men and women to make them slaves; and the Bible clearly suggests that slavery is inconsistent with human dignity—Noll argues that the abolitionists were hindered by many Christians' discomfort with arguments that could not be linked to an explicit directive in the biblical text.[23] Any way you look at it, Christians share some of the blame for the greatest blot on American history. But it is Christians who warped the teachings of their faith, not Christianity, that bear the blame.

This point was perhaps best made by an African American clergyman named Howard Thurman more than eighty years ago. During a visit by Thurman to India, a Hindu scholar called him "a traitor to all the darker peoples of earth" for embracing a religion whose practitioners had participated in and defended the slavery of Thurman's own forefathers. "I am wondering," the scholar said skeptically, "what you, an intelligent man, can say in defense of your position." Thurman did not offer a one-word response. Over the course of the next five hours, he pointed out that Jesus himself was a "poor Jew" and "a member of a minority group in the midst of a larger dominant and controlling group"—the Roman Empire. "The basic fact," Thurman told the Hindu scholar,

> is that Christianity as it was born in the mind of this Jewish teacher and thinker appears as a technique of survival for the oppressed. That it became, through the intervening years, a religion of the powerful and the dominant, used sometimes

as an instrument of oppression, must not tempt us into believing it was thus in the mind and life of Jesus. "In him was life; and the life was the light of men."

The evil done by Christians was not a weakness of his religion, Thurman concluded, but "a betrayal of the genius of that religion."[24]

A World of Testimonies

There is another way to consider the uniqueness of Christianity's explanation of our idea-making capacity. I argued earlier that any religion or system of thought that claims to be true should be able to show how its adherents' lives have been transformed. The testimonies I described came from the United States and England. But the testimonies of a religion or system of thought that is universally true should not be limited to a particular place or time or ethnic group. This, too, is what we see with Christianity.

In every era, people in every place that Christianity has touched testify that it has transformed their lives. This can be hard for those of us who live in the West to appreciate, since Christianity has been a familiar presence for so long. But there are far more new testimonies of the goodness of Christianity in China or Africa than in all of the Western nations combined. In 1955, Africa had an estimated sixteen million Catholics; the number today is roughly 170 million.[25] In China, a house-church movement—in which Christian groups hold worship services in their homes, often featuring music, preaching and testimonies of Christians recounting how their conversion to Christianity has transformed their lives— has swept the country, initially reaching the lower and middle classes and more recently making significant inroads among

China's cultural elites. Two of the twenty-one best-known leaders of the Tiananmen Square protests are now ordained priests.[26]

Let me be clear that I am not talking primarily about the numerical growth of Christianity, although the numbers are impressive. What is remarkable is the diversity of contexts in which people have embraced the ideals of Christianity. Many of these people who are convinced that Christianity is true are poor, but others are wealthy. In countries where Christianity is forcibly excluded, as in China or Russia in the twentieth century or in large parts of the Middle East today, it is sometimes kept at bay for a time. But it rarely disappears, and as soon as there is an opening, we usually see a surge in testimonies from those whose lives have been transformed by Christianity. In a remarkable number of cases, the transformation comes simply from reading the Bible, before the person ever meets another Christian.

Perhaps materialism will one day have a similar effect, with men and women in every nation saying that they once were blind but now they see or that they have pulled themselves up from the gutter as a result of its teachings. But this hasn't happened yet. The testimonies of the adherents of some religions—most notably, Islam—are more impressive and pervasive. But if we took a close look at each, I think we would conclude that Christianity is unique in the range of societies in which these testimonies can be found.

The testimonies do not prove that Christianity is true, but they are further evidence that Christianity has credible explanations for humans' most puzzling feature: our capacity and compulsion to make and debate ideas about the universe and our place in it. Christians believe that our idea-making capacity is not accidental—

it matters—and that it enables us, both as individuals and collectively, to better navigate a universe that is the reflection of the God who made it. The practical usefulness of mathematics hints that "something has gotten our minds into immediate contact with the rational order of the world."[27] Even Christianity's most controversial feature, its ideas about ethics, has the qualities we would expect from a set of ideas that could be true.

A few years ago, Jordan Monge arrived at Harvard for her freshman year. Raised in Orange County, California, she was the atheist daughter of an atheist philosopher. "Why would I believe in God?" she recalled to a reporter for the *Harvard Crimson*.[28] "There's no evidence for God." But she was haunted by the mysteries of our idea-making capacity. She believed that there must be some universal truths—what philosophers call "mind independent values"—and she believed in human rights, "but couldn't really give an explanation as to why."

A friend pushed her on these issues as they sat on futons in empty practice rooms in Harvard's music building. As she investigated the "rich tradition of Christian intellect," she concluded that "the only reasonable course of action was to believe in the death and resurrection of Jesus."[29] "This walk has proved to be quite a journey," she wrote in a first-person account of these and other factors that led her to embrace Christianity, "but I have committed to follow the way of Christ wherever it may lead. When confronted with the overwhelming body of evidence I encountered, when facing down the living God, it was the only rational course of action."[30]

2

BEAUTY AND THE ARTS

Many years ago, after my sophomore year in college, two friends and I spent the summer hitchhiking around the West Coast. They left for home before I did, so I found myself hitchhiking north of San Francisco by myself at the end of the summer. Several days later, as I was walking along a mountain road in the redwood region shortly after dawn, feeling sorry for myself after having spent the previous night shivering in my sleeping bag by the side of the road, a break in the trees gave me an unexpected view of the valley below. The valley was covered with a layer of clouds and fog that nestled among the trees and seemed to glow in the early morning light. It was as if I'd been transported to Shangri-La. I was overwhelmed by the beauty and felt a deep sense of joy, but both were immediately tempered by the sadness of knowing that the initial euphoria would soon pass.

Each of us has had experiences like this one. The sense of joy and the accompanying sense of sadness are features that men and women of all times and places have associated with beauty.

In the late nineteenth century, many Americans had almost the same Shangri-La experience without even going outside, much less traveling from one side of the country to the other. A group of painters who became known as the Hudson River School—because several lived near the Hudson River in New York and it inspired many of their paintings—painted spectacular landscapes of mountains, gorges and woods on enormous canvases. Among the most revered of these painters were Thomas Cole, Frederic Edwin Church and Albert Bierstadt. The paintings were so popular that some went on tour. A traveling carnival might include entertainers, a bearded woman and a tent with a new, "never before seen" Hudson River School painting. Newspapers reported that, when viewers poked their heads inside and got their first glimpse of the painting—its wonders enhanced by suitably dramatic lighting—there were loud gasps.

I was reminded of this when I visited the Detroit Institute of Arts recently and saw one of the Hudson River School paintings. The painting was admirable, but neither I nor anyone else in the room was overcome. I was more taken by a less dramatic landscape by the seventeenth-century Dutch painter Jacob van Ruisdael, which portrayed a soothing rustic scene punctuated by a few faintly ominous dead branches, and even more by the blues and violets and syncopated space in a painting of the interior of a room by the early twentieth-century French artist Henri Matisse.

We don't always agree about what is and isn't beautiful. What some experience as beautiful, others may see as a waste of canvas. And conventions about beauty change through time. If this were not the case, Rubens's fleshy nudes would seem as beautiful to us today as they did in his own day, and billionaires would bid fortunes for scenes of Venice by Canalleto rather than Picasso or Jasper Johns paintings. Yet everyone experiences *some* art as beautiful, and we can probably agree on many of the attributes of beauty, even if we disagree about what is beautiful.

The same is true of music, ballet and other arts. When Stravinsky's *Rite of Spring* was first performed in Paris in 1913, a minor riot ensued and a portion of the audience stampeded out. Yet many music lovers now find *Rite of Spring*'s discordance hauntingly beautiful.

Our sense of beauty is thus connected with our idea-making capacity. "The more you know about wine, the better it tastes," I once heard a wine expert say. The same can be true of art. We can learn to appreciate art that initially makes no impression on us, perhaps because its conventions are literally or figuratively foreign. But there are important differences too. Beauty has a physical effect on us that ideas alone ordinarily do not, an admixture of longing and a sense that beauty is not as enduring as it should be. This perception that beauty is real and that it reflects the universe as it is meant to be, but that it is impermanent and somehow corrupted, is the paradox of beauty. Any religion or system of thought that claims to be true needs to shed light on this paradox.

The Materialist Answers

How does materialism explain the role that beauty plays in our lives? Well over a century ago, Charles Darwin asked this question. He started with the puzzle of beauty in the animal world. Why, he asked, do animals develop beautiful but seemingly useless features, such as an Irish elk's spectacular antlers or the peacock's elaborate tail? The idea of natural selection doesn't have much to offer here, since these features are more likely to hinder than help the elk's or the peacock's survival.

Darwin solved this problem by devising a complementary theory he called sexual selection.[1] Although the antlers and iridescent tail didn't protect elks and peacocks against predators or other threats, they did help to attract females. Because elks with larger antlers or peacocks with more colorful tails were more likely to find mates and produce offspring, these traits would be favored, and antlers and tails would become increasingly spectacular over time.

Although sexual selection provided a plausible explanation for the peacock's tail, it cannot be the reason we find a painting by Rembrandt or Renoir beautiful, or tingle at the sight of a sunset over the ocean. Unlike with animals, as Darwin himself acknowledged, our sense of beauty involves "complex ideas and trains of thought." As he put it, "When . . . it is said that the lower animals have a sense of beauty, it must not be supposed that such sense is comparable with that of a cultivated man, with his multiform and complex associated ideas."[2] Beauty, in other words, is a lot more complicated with us.

This is more or less where Darwin left things. Natural and sexual selection did not provide a golden key to the mystery of beauty. Contemporary materialists have tended to explain our experience of beauty in one of two ways. Some materialists dismiss our love of art as an accident of our humanness. Stephen Jay Gould, a well-known Harvard paleontologist and popularizer of Darwinian insights, called art a "spandrel" in human evolution, analogizing it to the triangular space between an arch and the rectangular framework that houses the arch in a medieval building.[3] Spandrels are attractive and a magnet for decoration, but they are unnecessary to the structure of the building. In the same way, Gould argued, art is simply a byproduct of our unusually large brain. Although many aspects of our mental capacity helped us to survive, our desire to make and appreciate art was not one of them. Steven Pinker has made a similar point. "The mind is a neural computer," he says. "It is driven by goal states that served biological fitness in ancestral environments. . . . That toolbox, however, can be used to assemble Sunday afternoon projects of dubious adaptive value."[4]

It is possible that our experience of beauty is an accidental byproduct, just as it is possible that our idea-making capacity is accidental. But there is something deeply unsatisfying about this dismissal of our subjective experience of beauty. Beauty is central to our experience as humans. It seems unlikely that a feature that has always seemed so essential to our lives is a fluke, simply an extra tool in the toolkit.

A second group of materialists takes the opposite tack, trying to explain why art and our experience of beauty may be adaptive for human beings. The theories are wide ranging. Some materialists have speculated that the visceral reaction we experience when we see a particularly beautiful vista in nature may have given human beings who had this trait a leg up because it alerted them to the prospect of food. Pinker himself hints at this perspective in places. "We pay attention to features of the visual world that signal safe, unsafe, or changing habitats, such as distant views, greenery, gathering clouds, and sunsets."[5] He bases this conclusion in part on a survey of gardeners', photographers' and painters' perceptions of beauty. "The landscapes thought to be loveliest are dead ringers for an optimal savanna."[6]

Other materialists argue that art helps to promote social cohesion. We are "wired for culture," according to one advocate of this perspective, Mark Pagel. "Music, dance, religion, and even laughter [are] aids to promoting the sense of group membership and mutual well-being that gives rise to . . . self-sacrificial emotions."[7] A shared appreciation of art would encourage solidarity within a community, the reasoning goes, which would increase the likelihood of survival.

The speculation that beautiful landscapes signaled to our ancient forebears that food might be nearby has the hallmarks of an initial stab in the dark. The moments when we stand in stunned silence before a sublime vista have almost precisely the opposite effect than a real signal that food is nearby. The British Romantic poets of the nineteenth century, who were fascinated by our sense of the sublime in nature, treated these encounters as moments of hushed introspection. The narrator in a William Wordsworth poem says, "I have felt / A presence that disturbs me with the joy / Of elevated thoughts, a sense sublime / Of something far more deeply interfused, / Whose dwelling is the light of setting suns, / And the round ocean and the living air."[8] Like Wordsworth's narrator, most of us are inclined to forget about food as we admire the forest or other vista, not to race forward in order to search among the trees. Even after the moment of splendor passes, we are as likely to turn away from the landscape as to attempt to enter it.

The theory that art induces social cohesion is not quite so implausible, but it doesn't quite seem to work either. Art sometimes can have a unifying effect in a society. When Americans see the famous painting of George Washington crossing the Delaware River or sing the national anthem, most feel a sense of solidarity with the nation. Other countries have their own iconic paintings or anthems. The close links between a nation and its art are one of the reasons that countries like Italy, Greece and Turkey have so strenuously campaigned for the return of antiquities that have wound up in museums or private collections in other countries.

Yet social cohesion is only one of the dimensions of art and hardly its most telling or pervasive attribute, especially in the modern era. Art often serves to isolate us from those around us, rather than to strengthen the ties that bind us together. The alienated artist is a modern cliché, but it nevertheless reflects a genuine reality about art. Even if one does not thumb her nose at conventional culture, as the French poet Baudelaire did; simply disappear, as did Rimbaud; or revel in countercultural excesses, like Allen Ginsberg and the American Beat poets, art often is sparked by the friction between the artist and society. A poet friend of mine insists that art and the artist must always be marginal. This perhaps overstates the case, but even the most well-adjusted and sociable artists generally make their art in isolation, and many are not notably successful in passing their genes down to future generations.

Something similar holds true for those of us who listen to or view art. Our first and primary reaction to a Matisse painting or a Bach concerto is personal, not communal, much as with a beautiful landscape. Often the effect is most powerful when it cannot be fully shared, either because we are alone or because the art does not have quite the same effect on those around us.

Although evolutionary psychologists do not yet have a plausible explanation for our sense of beauty, experimental scientists have made better progress studying how beauty and other intense emotional experiences affect our brains. With modern imaging techniques, scientists increasingly can trace our thoughts or emotions to activity in particular regions of the brain. The uncanny ability of the Grammy-award-winning pop vocalist Adele to bring audiences to tears is an intriguing recent example. Using Adele's song "Someone Like You," a science writer attempted to pinpoint the qualities that produce its intense emotional effect. Of particular note in "Someone Like You," he concluded, is the use of "ornamental notes that clash with the melody just enough to create a dissonant sound."[9] According to a psychologist who has studied music's physiological effects, the pattern of tension and release provokes an emotional response, especially if it occurs several times in succession. Other scientists, including a group of neuroscientists at McGill University, report that dopamine floods into the pleasure quadrant of our brains when we listen to emotionally intense music.

As fascinating as the new brain studies are, they are far cruder than the breathless reports of new findings sometimes suggest. As my colleague Stephen Morse (a materialist, I should perhaps add) often points out, current brain imaging can identify only broad patterns in brain response.[10] It doesn't have anything like the pinpoint accuracy that enthusiasts sometimes claim. Perhaps would-be songwriters will benefit from the knowledge that a succession of moments of tension and release in a song can produce goose bumps, for instance, but this is hardly a guarantee that a song will bring tears to its listeners' eyes.

The new neuroscience has another limitation as well. Thus far, at least, it doesn't offer any guidance on the one aspect of beauty we care most about: the sense that beauty gives us a glimpse into the true nature of the universe, a glimpse that is both temporary and real, and which suggests that the world is not as it should be. Like the theories of the evolutionary psychologists, the neuroscientists' findings do not give us clues as to why beauty has such a puzzling effect on us. The goose bumps are only on the surface; the real mystery is the meaning we attach to the experience that produces them.

Please do not mistake the nature of the claim I am making here. I am not suggesting that materialists will never devise a plausible explanation for the mystery of beauty or for other dimensions of our subjective experience. Perhaps in time they will. New scientific studies may give materialists new ideas in the future. But the current materialist explanations are notably thin. They flatten out the complexity of beauty and describe something that most of us do not recognize as its essence.

Pantheist and Dualist Perspectives

If materialism falls short, at least for now, can religious accounts better explain the paradox of beauty? If we turned this into a true-false question, the answer probably would be "true," since transcendence is central both to our experience of beauty and to nearly every human religion. But religions vary dramatically in their understanding of beauty. To see this, we need to distinguish among three different conceptions of a spiritual dimension in the universe: pantheism, dualism and Christianity. (Christianity shares some features with Judaism and Islam, but differs importantly from both, especially Islam, in its explanation of beauty.)

Start with pantheism. Pantheists believe that spiritual forces are woven into the very fabric of the universe. The term *pantheism* is somewhat unfortunate, because it calls up images of distant, seemingly primitive tribes who worship trees and stones and who seem far removed from modern secular life. But the sophisticated classical Greek philosophy called Stoicism was pantheistic, as are many contemporary forms of spirituality, such as the New Age movement. Pantheists believe that divinity is ubiquitous, residing within us (the New Age emphasis) and throughout the world. If it were possible to take a Gallup poll of worldviews through all of history, pantheism might well come out on top.

In one very important sense, the pantheistic worldview is true to our experience of beauty. If everything around us is divine, the wonder when we encounter a beautiful vista or brilliant work of art is perfectly understandable. The poet Gerald Manley Hopkins wrote as a Christian, not a pantheist, when he marveled that "the world is charged with the grandeur of God," and "there lives the dearest freshness deep down things." But a pantheist could fully endorse this praise for the world around us. If everything is divine, it is no wonder we greet the sunrise with awe.

Although pantheism seems to better explain the wonder we feel in the presence of beauty than materialism, like materialism it falters in the face of beauty's paradoxical qualities. If everything genuinely is divine, why are the bursts of beauty we experience so intermittent and short lived? Perhaps if we were pantheists, we would begin to encounter the divine in everything, no matter how ordinary or ungainly. But it seems more likely that the universal experience of beauty as real but incomplete, as something we know only in glimpses, is not mistaken. It reflects a quality of beauty that pantheist religions have difficulty explaining.

A much more serious limitation emerges when we consider the other great puzzle of beauty: our sense that the beauty we experience is not only temporary, it also is frequently corrupted by ugliness and horror. Pantheism does not give us a way to make sense of evil, either in general or as it infects beauty. Some pantheists suggest that ugliness and evil do not exist or that they can be dissolved. This is a frequent strategy of New Age thinkers, who invite their advocates to tap into healing forces. Other pantheists, including the ancient Stoics, treat ugliness as inextricably linked to the divine forces that pervade everything. We're simply stuck with ugliness and evil, they believed. Neither explains why ugliness and horror seem both real (contrary to New Age pantheism) and wrong (contrary to Stoicism), warping a world that might otherwise be full of the beauty we experience only in glimpses now.

Like pantheism, dualism has a long and varied pedigree in human history. According to one form of dualism, a god or gods exist, but their realm is entirely separate from human existence. This form of dualism is familiar to most Americans as the deism espoused by Thomas Jefferson and some of the other founding fathers—probably including George Washington, despite the heroic efforts of a few recent writers to turn him into a traditional Christian. According to the deists, an all-powerful god created Earth and the rest of the universe, but the creator stands off at a distance and does not take an active interest in the ordinary affairs of men and women.

Deism traces back historically to another group of ancient Greeks, the Epicureans, who held very similar views. Although Epicureans believed in gods, rather than a single God, they too believed that deities keep their distance from human activities. As Epicurus himself put it in the first of his *Principal Doctrines*, "What is blessed and immortal neither has troubles itself nor causes them for another, and accordingly is not affected either by anger or favor."[11]

When it comes to beauty, deism more closely resembles materialism than any of the other religious perspectives. Because spiritual affairs are so far removed from our daily existence, according to deists, they do not figure in a deist understanding of beauty. As with materialism, deism does not explain beauty's most maddening, saddening and deeply characteristic quality: the sense that it gives us a glimpse into the true nature of the universe, a glimpse that is both temporary and real and that suggests the world is not as it should be.

The other form of dualism draws a slightly different line. For these dualists, the key distinction is not so much between realms that are nearby or far off—our earthly existence here and the spiritual realm in some far-off there—as between spirit and matter. Plato is the best-known early advocate of spirit-matter dualism, as in his arguments that earthly objects are imperfect approximations of a more perfect spiritual form. A table or chair, for instance, corresponds imperfectly to the ideal form of a table or chair. In the religious version of spirit-matter dualism, which is generally called Gnosticism, matter is often viewed as not only inferior to spirit but also as evil. Early Gnostics believed that good and evil forces vied for control of the universe and that the evil forces are responsible for the created world.

Although the number of people who would identify themselves as Gnostics in the contemporary world is small, Gnosticism has had, and still has, an influence far exceeding its numbers. St. Augustine was tempted by spirit-matter dualism and in fact followed a Gnostic movement during his twenty- and thirty-something years. C. S. Lewis was similarly tempted. "I freely admit," he wrote in *Mere Christianity*, "that real Christianity . . . goes much nearer to Dualism than people think."[12] Gnosticism is a familiar feature of American popular culture—as in the *Star Wars* movies—and the literary critic Harold Bloom once claimed that it is the most important and most distinctively American religion.[13]

Part of spirit-matter dualism's appeal is that it does explain central features of our experience, such as the paradox of beauty, far better than the other perspectives we have seen. If matter is evil, as spirit-matter dualists claim, we should not be surprised that our glimpses of beauty are fleeting and often obscured by ugliness and horror.

The problem with this dualist conception is that it subtly but decisively mischaracterizes the nature of the longing we feel in the presence of great art or memorable scenery. We do not long to be spirited away from where we are, into an altogether different realm. We do not long to leave at all. We long for the material world, the world we live in, to be transformed, and for the sense of transcendence to endure.

This is the place where Christianity parts company with dualism. According to Christianity, the vista that takes our breath away isn't evil; it's good. Ordinary matter and the physical world aren't evil either. We're told this seven different times in the first chapter of the Bible—that the earth is good, that vegetation is good, that the sun, moon and stars are good, and so on. In contrast to dualism, Christianity explains the paradox of beauty as our recognition that the world around us is good but it has been corrupted. The ugliness isn't inherent, and in fact it doesn't belong.

The Christian Alternative

Christianity teaches that we experience all of these things when we marvel at a Matisse painting or stand speechless before a stunning landscape. Beauty points beyond the creation, as dualism claims, but it also is a feature of the material world. This world is not as it should be; it has been bent and corrupted. We long for it to be transformed.

For a materialist, this may sound like a lot of wishful thinking. What Christians really long for is heaven, a materialist might say, and they smuggle this longing into their understanding of beauty. What Christians call beauty is really just the words of Christians who look at the world with heaven-colored glasses.

But this objection cannot be right. Materialists themselves are the best evidence that we are wired to experience this sense of transcendence. If beauty has no real connection with transcendence, we would expect materialists to be immune from the potent mix of emotions the rest of us feel in the presence of beauty. After all, materialists are convinced that God and heaven do not exist. But materialists are not immune at all. Perhaps there are exceptions, but materialists have the same appreciation for beauty and experience the same emotions in its presence as everyone else. The composer Leonard Bernstein once said that when he listened to the music of Bach, he thought for a moment that there must be a God. Materialist astronomers gape in wonder at some of the images of the cosmos produced by the most powerful telescopes. These reactions are just what a Christian conception of our place in the universe would lead us to expect.

These comments about the general paradox of beauty are sufficient to make my key claim: that the Christian explanation is true to the reality of our experience of beauty in ways that materialist and other religious alternatives are not. But I believe that the Christian understanding can tell us even more about our experience of beauty; it helps to explain why we find certain qualities beautiful in poetry and other arts.

Christianity and Beauty

Mark Twain once said that a first-rate mind has the ability to hold two opposing ideas at the same time. Many of the best-known poems are based on something like this principle. When Robert Frost's poem "The Road Not Taken" speaks of coming to a fork in the road and taking "the road less traveled," we immediately recognize that the narrator of the poem is engaged in two different journeys, one literal and the other metaphorical. When a character in a Shakespeare play talks about dying, it's often in the form of an extended pun linking death and sex.

In the middle of the twentieth century, a group of poets and literary critics whose movement became known as New Criticism insisted that all true poems have these qualities. They argued, as one retrospective puts it, that "the most mature literary art [is] not content to associate like with like but [seeks] to bring into meaningful relation materials that we commonly think of as quite unlike."[14] In the most beautiful poems, the ideas are teased out and somehow knit together without losing the distinctiveness of each. In "Ode on a Grecian Urn," by early nineteenth-century English poet John Keats, a favorite of the New Critics, the figures frolicking on the urn will never die, but they will never complete their games. And Keats treats them as if they were real, while also reminding the reader that they are simply figures painted on an urn.

Although other tenets of New Criticism have been rightly criticized, and there are few tenured New Critics today, the observation that tension—and often paradox—is a key feature of beautiful art seems to be universally true. The tension may come from colors or shapes that pull in opposing directions rather than ideas, and there is more to beauty than tension alone; but brilliantly managed tension is a common theme that links together art that is perceived as beautiful.

The philosopher Nicholas Wolterstorff defines the key features of art in a different but analogous fashion. According to Wolterstorff, there are three dimensions of aesthetic quality: unity, internal richness and intensity of fittingness.[15] The unity of a poem or work of art is its proportion or symmetry (Leonardo da Vinci's famous drawing of a man was intended to show the symmetry of the parts of a man's body). By intensity of fittingness, Wolterstorff means qualities like delicacy, tenderness or gracefulness. Internal richness corresponds closely to the New Critics' love of paradox. The internal richness of a poem or work of art is its complexity and use of variation. Artists have this quality in mind when they say that the colors or imagery in a painting do or don't "move." The theme and variations in a musical composition contribute to its internal richness, as do the paradoxical features of a Keats poem.

Notice the similarities between the qualities I have just described and the emotions we experience in the presence of natural beauty. Although our reaction to a beautiful landscape is different in some respects from our appreciation of great art (you don't need an art history course to be awed by a sunset, for instance), beauty is accompanied by a sense of tension or paradox in each context.

At this point, I want to make and then defend a strong claim: Christianity provides a uniquely satisfying explanation of why we find these particular qualities so alluring. Even if you doubt that Christianity could possibly be true, I hope you will agree that it offers a surprisingly apt explanation of the features that make great art distinctive.

Christians believe that the sensations we associate with beauty reflect the deepest reality of our existence: that we are finite but made in the image of a transcendent God and that we long for him and yet have rebelled against him. As with our idea-making capacity, the only other religions or theories of reality that explain in similar terms what it means to be human are Judaism and Islam. All three can explain the wonder we feel in the presence of natural beauty.

But Christianity better explains the paradoxical qualities we associate with beauty more fully than the other monotheistic religions, because these same qualities lie at the very heart of Christianity. To show what I mean by this, we need to take a brief foray into Christian theology.

Christians believe that Jesus, who died so that we might be reconciled with God, was fully human and fully God. This seems impossible, and even Christians do not claim to fully understand what it means, but it is impossible in the same (or at least in a similar) way that the most spectacular art is impossible. If Jesus is indeed God, as Christians believe, this suggests that God somehow has both a "father" dimension and a "son" dimension. Christians believe that God has a "spirit" dimension as well, and thus that God is a "trinity." These dimensions, which Christians believe to be distinct persons, are quite different. The Son is obedient to the Father, for instance, and the Spirit nearly always directs our attention to the Son, even though they all are a single God.

That was a lot of theology in a single paragraph. St. Augustine devoted an entire (quite beautiful) philosophical treatise to the mysteries of the Trinity.[16] But the important point is that the creative tension among the three dimensions of God, and the paradox that God is both unity and diversity, is very similar to the qualities that we associate with a beautiful painting or concerto. Christians believe that this is not an accident and that it should not be a surprise that the beauty in a universe that was intended to be beautiful directly reflects the complexities of its Creator. To paraphrase a point made by the theologian N. T. Wright in another context, great art reflects the Creator back to himself.[17]

Let me pause here to address an objection you may have. If Christianity best explains our general sense of beauty and the qualities we find most beautiful, shouldn't Christians be the finest artists, since they most accurately grasp the nature of reality? Do I really think Christian artists are invariably the best? And if they aren't, doesn't this suggest that the Christian explanation of beauty is considerably less compelling than I've contended?

The short answer is that, even if Christianity offers the most compelling explanation of beauty, this does not mean that Christian artists will produce the finest art. As anyone who has encountered contemporary Christian music can attest, Christians are responsible for a great deal of highly inferior art. One reason for this seems to be a tendency in the past generation, at least in the West, for Christian artists to copy or critique rather than to create, as one cultural critic puts it.[18]

Another answer is that in art, as in other vocations, gifts are unequally distributed. When God gave Moses instructions for constructing a tabernacle for worship during Israel's wanderings in the desert, he singled out two particular people, named Bezalel and Oholiab, as the craftsmen who should oversee the work (Exodus 31:1-3, 6). Presumably, there were many other artists in Israel who were not quite so talented.

In addition, Christian artists sometimes write or paint or sing as if the tensions of our existence have been resolved. That is, an artist may call himself or herself Christian, yet produce art that is not true to reality as we experience it. The failure to engage the complexity of our existence can mar even the work of supremely gifted artists. The contemporary Christian artist Thomas Kinkade painted glowing, intricately detailed landscapes, often with cottages or rustic homes. As the art critic Daniel Siedell has written, the paintings invite Kinkade's "clientele to escape into an imaginary world where things can be pretty good, as long as we have our faith, our family values, and a visual imagery that re-affirms all this at the office and at home."[19] Although the paintings are very popular, they deny a central dimension of our experience: the ugliness and horror that so often accompany beauty. (This wasn't accidental; Kinkade once said, "I like to portray a world without the Fall.") Despite Kinkade's immense talent, his paintings do not have the kind of creative tension we associate with great art.

If we limit our focus to artists and works that nearly everyone considers to be great, we find many Christian artists, but also many artists who are not. For every deeply Christian artistic genius like Bach or the Renaissance painter Fra Angelico, we have equally brilliant non-Christian counterparts like Picasso or Stravinsky, or adherents of other religions such as the great Chinese poets of the Tang dynasty, starting in the seventh century. Are the great Christian artists somehow superior to the greats who were not Christian? The answer once again is no. Because Christian and non-Christian artists experience and respond to the same longing for beauty, it is no surprise that Christian artists do not have a monopoly on great art.

Although I do not claim any special connection between Christians and great art, I do claim that the most beautiful and memorable art will reflect the tensions and complexity that only Christianity can fully explain. Even the great art of artists who explicitly reject Christianity will have these features. The narrator of "Dover Beach," an 1867 poem by British poet Matthew Arnold, imagines the decline of the Sea of Faith, which was "once . . . at the full, and round earth's shore / Lay like the folds of a bright girdle furled." "But now," the narrator reports, "I only hear / Its melancholy, long, withdrawing roar, / Retreating." Although it has not proven prescient, the poem beautifully manages the interplay between the literal sights and sounds of the waves on the shore of Dover Beach as the tide recedes on the one hand and the intangible slipping away of faith on the other.

The abstract art of the past century emphasized color and line rather than recognizable faces or scenes, but it, too, is an art of internal richness and tensions. One prominent artist, Hans Hofmann, taught his students to aim for a "push-pull" effect, in which the colors and shapes seemed both to move toward the viewer and to recede from view, creating a dynamic tension. For those who prefer more traditional, representational art, Michelangelo espoused very similar artistic values for the figures in his paintings and sculptures. His figures often seem to strain in opposing directions, leaning back while pointing forward, as do Adam and God at the spark of creation depicted on the ceiling of the Sistine Chapel.

While we do not need any special training to gasp in wonder at a spectacular vista, we may not fully appreciate the intricacies of an Arnold poem, a Hoffman painting or a Chinese landscape without the experience or training to alert us to its nuances. Some art that others find beautiful may not move us in the same way. But we all find some things beautiful. When we do, the beauty we experience echoes the tensions at the heart of our existence.

Beauty and Truth

At the end of "Ode on a Grecian Urn," a poem by John Keats, the narrator concludes, "'Beauty is truth, truth beauty'—that is all / Ye know on earth, and all Ye need to know."[20] We have no way of knowing for sure whether Keats intended to embrace these lines as his poetic manifesto—to proclaim beauty as the only thing that matters—or whether they are implicitly ironic, given that the artist who made the urn died centuries ago. One reason the lines, and Keats's intent, have fascinated readers for two hundred years is that we are never quite sure whether beauty is related to truth.

If pressed, many modern Americans might conclude that it isn't. We tend to think of truth as objective statements about the world, shorn of any connection with beauty. But there are at least two ways in which beauty is indeed linked to truth.

The first is that beauty often creates a desire for truth. In the words of the Harvard aesthetician Elaine Scarry, "the beautiful person or thing incites in us the longing for truth."[21] It "prompts the mind to move chronologically back in the search for precedents and parallels, to move forward into new acts of creation, to move conceptually over, to bring things into relation, and does all this with a kind of urgency as though one's life depended on it." In this sense, beauty is not itself truth, but it sharpens our commitment to truth. Beauty often inspires a sense of conviction, which is, to quote Scarry again, "so pleasurable a mental state . . . that ever afterwards one is willing to labor, struggle, wrestle with the world to locate enduring sources of conviction—to locate what is true."[22] This is why many of us find ourselves making vows—often a vow to try to live a life of integrity—after we have an experience of beauty.

The second link is more direct. Some truths can only be conveyed, or are conveyed more effectively, through beauty. A psychology textbook may teach us a great deal about the psychological effects of intrafamily manipulation. But it can't teach us everything, as anyone who has spent a few hours reading *King Lear* will understand.

I have always suspected that this is why the Christian Scriptures are an artistic compilation of so many literary genres. Some parts of the Bible read like an instruction manual. Other parts are historical, recounting the reigns of Israel's kings in all their solemnity and farce. Each of the hundred and fifty psalms is a poem, as are Song of Solomon and snippets of the New Testament. The Bible also features proverbs and, in Jesus' teachings especially, parables.

A materialist philosopher friend of mine recently dismissed the Bible as the handiwork of unsophisticated Bronze Age writers, a view that is widely shared in some circles. Some, perhaps even many, of the Bible's writers may have been unsophisticated by modern standards, but the Bible itself is not. It is a work of startling literary beauty.

Robert Alter, a Hebrew and comparative literature scholar at the University of California, is perhaps the finest contemporary guide to its beauty. He has translated substantial portions of the Old Testament, including Genesis and the Psalms, with a particular sensitivity to the literary qualities of the text. For instance, in the story of Joseph, who was sold into slavery by his brothers and later rose to prominence in Egypt, Alter traces the use of hand metaphors—as in one brother's entreaty that the others not lay a hand on Joseph. When the wife of Joseph's Egyptian master attempts to seduce him, Joseph flees, "[leaving] his garment in her hand." Elsewhere in Genesis, leaving something in someone's hands is used as a metaphor for stewardship.

"A kind of dialectic is created," Alter concludes, "in the thematic unfolding of the story between hand as the agency of violent impulse and hand as the instrument of scrupulous management."[23] Alter is not a religious believer himself. But during a public conversation with the novelist Marilynne Robinson after his translation of the Psalms was published, he remarked that the Bible is so beautiful he sometimes finds himself wondering if it might be true.

My own first step toward embracing Christianity came at the outset of the same trip that landed me on the highway north of San Francisco. In my literature classes, we often read works with biblical references. Not having been raised in a religious environment of any kind, I never recognized any of the references. I decided I should at least read the Bible, so that I would better understand what I was reading. So I started at Genesis in the back of the borrowed van we drove across the country.

I was blown away. The raw psychological honesty of the Bible's portrayal of its major figures had the ring of truth. I hadn't expected the profusion of genres or the power and elegance of the overarching narrative that we repeatedly go astray yet God loves us and longs to take us back. In the years since, I have spent far more time thinking about other dimensions of Christianity, such as its explanations of the puzzles and paradoxes we have been exploring. And my own embrace of Christianity had several other stages. But the sheer beauty of the Bible is what first drew me in, and it's still what I go back to when I'm asked over a beer late at night why I believe that Christianity is true.

■ ■ ■

There is one dimension of beauty that we have not yet considered: beauty as experienced by those who are involved in the act of creation. The poet Randall Jarrell famously said that writing poetry is like standing outside in the rain for long periods, hoping to be struck by lightning. The movie *Amadeus* nicely portrays this feature of Mozart's creative process. As Mozart is dying, he dictates his Requiem Mass in D Minor to his disguised competitor, Salieri. Salieri watches in wonder each time Mozart enters a short phase of creative intensity of a kind that seems to have been continuous when Mozart was healthy. The psychologist Mihaly Csikszentmihalyi calls these periods of creative transcendence "flow," the sense some artists have of being in a zone where they lose all track of time and where they feel they're doing what they're created to do.[24]

As brain-imaging technology continues to improve, we may be able to track the shifts that take place in the brain when artists experience this sense of flow. Indeed, some scientists purport to have tracked the changes in the brains of men and women as they entered the state of heightened consciousness that comes with meditation.[25] Capturing images of an artist's brain at the moment creative lightning strikes is at least imaginable. But even if we could describe what happens, this would not tell us what it means, what the significance of these moments of artistic intensity is.

Christianity teaches that the sense of transcendence is a feature of our having been created in the image of God. God created the universe, and created it good. Because we are created in the image of the Creator, we too have an impulse to create. Even those of us who will never be in the zone that Jarrell or Mozart experienced are likely to have a desire to create in some way. Those who have genuine creative gifts and who dedicate themselves to the creative process as Jarrell and Mozart and the Bronze Age artisans Bezalel and Oholiab did may experience periods when they are in this transcendent zone.

As with the longing all of us experience in the presence of beauty, artists' experience of heightened creative inspiration is inevitably temporary. Christianity explains our inability to sustain transcendence as evidence that creation, and the creation, have been corrupted. But Christianity teaches that the moments of transcendence are more than simply chemical changes in our brains. They are hints that the universe is not as it is intended to be and as it will one day be. "It was when I was happiest that I longed most," the central character in C. S. Lewis's novel *Till We Have Faces* says as she reflects on her encounters with beauty. "And because it was beautiful, it set me longing, always longing. Somewhere else, there must be more of it."[26]

3

SUFFERING AND SENSATION

In early 2008, my dear friend Bill Stuntz, a criminal law and criminal procedure scholar the *New York Times* has described as "one of the most influential legal scholars of the past generation," learned that he had a large mass in his colon.[1] During an annual physical, the doctor had discovered that Bill was bleeding internally and probably had been for months. The doctor immediately ordered a biopsy. When the results came back, they confirmed that the large mass in Bill's colon was, as the doctor suspected, cancer.

There was a dark irony with the cancer. Bill had been in severe pain since December 31, 1999—his own personal Y2K, as he called it—when the base of his spine shifted while he was replacing a flat tire on his car at the end of a family vacation. The next eight years brought two major operations and a daily cocktail of drugs for the pain, but the pain in his back and right leg rarely eased. He lived with it and worked through it as best he could. It was, he said, as if an alarm clock that has been turned up to the highest volume was taped to his ear and he couldn't turn it off. He was forty-one years old when the ordeal began.

The irony is this: if Bill wasn't already in so much pain, he would have paid more attention to the discomfort he'd felt in his abdomen for months, and the cancer might have been discovered much sooner. But he didn't think anything of it. He assumed it was connected to his back pain or perhaps was a side effect of one of his medications.

I have a confession to make. While Bill was waiting for a definitive diagnosis, I found myself parsing our conversations for evidence that this awful sequence of events had shaken his Christian faith. I wondered if there might be a breaking point. I was afraid for Bill's body, I was afraid for his faith, and to be honest, I was afraid for me.

The question I was wrestling with is known as the "problem of evil." If a good God oversees the universe, why would he allow devastating hurricanes, senseless killings of schoolchildren and the kind of suffering Bill was enduring? Many skeptics of Christianity do not believe that Christianity can answer this question. They are right that this is the most difficult dilemma for Christianity. But Christianity does have an answer—an immensely practical one. It just isn't in the place where skeptics and many Christians tend to look for it.

The Problem of Evil

Unlike with idea making and beauty, nearly every other religion and system of thought seems to have a more compelling explanation for suffering than Christianity does. For a materialist,

Bill's back pain and cancer were simply part of the natural order. Pain is our bodies' alarm system, warning us that something is wrong and needs to be taken care of. It is an evolutionary adaptation that helped our ancestors to survive. If Bill's back problems were fixable, his pain would have done just what it was designed to do. The tragedy, a materialist would say, was that doctors could not remedy the back problem, and the pain became constant. Cancer also is part of the natural order. We don't know exactly how it emerged, but cancer has adapted to the physiology of humans and other animals.

Suffering is perhaps slightly more puzzling for pantheist religions, but for them, too, it is part of the natural order. Pantheists believe that suffering is inevitable and can't be eradicated, although they draw different implications from this. Stoics tended to see suffering as something to be endured (and suicide as the solution if it cannot be), whereas New Age spiritualists are often more optimistic about our ability to remove the source of the suffering.

Some Eastern religions—such as Hinduism, in some of its forms—teach that suffering is punishment for our sins in a previous life. From this perspective, suffering is part of a rational system of punishment and reward. It is completely understandable even if we cannot predict whether and when we will suffer.

Even a dualist religion like Gnosticism seems to more fully account for suffering than Christianity does. The Gnostics taught that the forces of good and evil do constant battle and that the good god has no part in the material world, which is evil. If the matter from which human beings are made is evil, the ubiquity of suffering is hardly surprising.

For Christianity, by contrast, which teaches that the universe was good when God created it and that suffering was not part of the natural order in the beginning, suffering is a great mystery. If a good God created the universe, where did evil come from and why didn't God prevent it? The philosopher David Hume famously said that if God is capable of preventing suffering but didn't, he is malevolent; and if he is willing to prevent suffering but incapable, he is impotent. God is either malevolent or impotent, Hume suggests, or he doesn't exist.[2] An atheist philosopher friend of mine poses the question this way: if God exists and is good, why didn't he create a world in which Hitler planted rows of tulips instead of murdering millions of Jews and other "undesirables"?

Christians have given several kinds of answers to questions like this. St. Augustine sought to exonerate God from the charge of being the author of evil through a careful definition of the relationship between good and evil. Everything that God created was good and could only be good, but it is possible for good to be corrupted. Evil is not separate from good, in the sense that some matter is good and other matter is evil. Evil is good that has been corrupted; it is the absence of good.[3]

This seems to me a very helpful way to understand evil, but it seems to make evil more passive than it is, and it still doesn't tell us why evil is possible in the first place. Here is the best answer I know, this time by way of C. S. Lewis. Lewis pointed out that if people are genuinely distinct from one another, as they must be if we are to have individual personalities, we must communicate through matter whose arrangement will not be equally pleasing to every one of us at all times. This creates opportunities for cooperation, but also for conflict. If we truly have freedom of choice as we respond to these differences—if we are not simply automatons—the possibility of evil is inevitable. The evil humans cause is a consequence of our free will.[4]

Perhaps you (unlike Lewis) can imagine a universe that has been exquisitely fine-tuned so that every person—roughly 7.2 billion at the moment—has free will and yet no one of them steps on the toes of any other. In this universe, Hitler does indeed plant rows of tulips. Or perhaps God or some other supernatural force miraculously intervenes each time a potential harm materializes, no matter how small. I myself cannot imagine such a universe, but it seems theoretically possible that a universe could be created in this fashion. Indeed, Christianity teaches that the afterlife will have many of these qualities. If such a universe comes readily to mind for you, you will not find the explanation of evil as an unavoidable side effect of free will especially compelling. You will continue to ask why God, if there is a God, created a universe in which men and women suffer.

Even for those of us who do find the free-will argument persuasive, or at least helpful, misuse of free will does not explain every dimension of evil. It tells us about the suffering men and women inflict on one another but much less about the horrors of nature. Misuse of free will does not explain the havoc that hurricanes and other natural disasters wreak on vulnerable populations or other atrocities of the natural world. This does not mean that there are no other explanations for the horrors of nature, of course—just that most of these horrors seem far removed from issues of human free will. A variety of explanations are indeed on offer from theologians of various stripes, including a much more sophisticated version of the free-will explanation of human evil that I just described—an argument based on the inevitable dislocations of a transition from chaos to order.

I will leave these speculations to others. I am confident that, if we worked our way through the panoply of possible explanations, we would conclude that, although some are better and some worse, they do not add up to a full answer to the problem of evil.

I should add one last dimension to this brief overview of the problem of evil. It is possible that what seems evil to us now, from our limited human perspective, is actually part of some greater good that we do not fully understand. When we question whether the evil and suffering in the world can be reconciled with the existence of God, we assume we are the measure of justice. There is a certain arrogance in this assumption. Humility suggests we should be open to the possibility that the evil we are familiar with might look different if we could see the entire course of future events, and if we knew the alternative possibilities of the past.

In the end, I do not think Christianity can give a complete explanation of *why* there is suffering and evil in the world. Nor do I say this solely on my own authority. Everyone who reads the book of Job notices that, although Job repeatedly asks God for an explanation of suffering and evil, God never gives him one. The Bible does teach that human evil is a consequence of our sin—that is, the misuse of free will by Adam and Eve, and by men and women ever since. But it does not fully explain where evil came from or whether it would be possible to create a universe in which men and women have free will but never misuse it.

This may seem like an odd concession to make. After all, the problem of evil is the biggest impediment to Christianity for many men and women. Nevertheless, I believe it is a necessary concession. And it has a very surprising consequence: once we have acknowledged that Christianity never fully explains why our lives are full of suffering and grief, we can begin to see how Christianity not only makes sense of suffering, but actually makes better sense of suffering than other religions or systems of thought. The contrast is once again starkest with materialism.

Puzzles for Materialists

Dating back to Darwin himself, materialists have often pointed to the ichneumon wasp—sometimes referred to as Darwin's wasp—as especially vivid evidence that the natural world could not have been created and overseen by a good God. To feed its larvae, the ichneumon wasp paralyzes a caterpillar and then lays eggs on it so that the wasp's larvae can slowly eat the caterpillar while the caterpillar is still alive. The larvae begin with the caterpillar's nonessential organs, saving its vital organs for last, so that the victim will stay alive as long as possible. A benign creator could never have allowed something this gruesome, the reasoning goes.

It's an awful scene, and it's hard not to agree with Richard Dawkins when he says that he hopes caterpillars are not capable of feeling pain.[5] But Dawkins's reaction is in one respect puzzling. Why does a materialist find the wasp's behavior troubling? After all, it's simply a strategy the wasp has evolved to feed its young. It is a part of the natural order. Yet it seems to make many materialists at least a little bit uncomfortable. Why is this? The most plausible answer is that some kinds of suffering seem wrong, even to a hard-boiled materialist and even when the behavior is adaptive.

Moral discomfort figures equally prominently in other illustrations materialists use to question the possibility of there being a good God. For Voltaire, the awful Lisbon earthquake of 1755 proved that God could not exist. "What crime, what sin," the narrator asks in "Poem on the Lisbon Disaster," "had those young hearts conceived / That lie, bleeding and torn, on mother's breast? / Did fallen Lisbon deeper drink of vice / Than London, Paris, or sunlit Madrid?" The earthquake seemed wrong to Voltaire, somehow evil, just as more recent disasters seem wrong to us today, even though they are part of the natural order.

Some materialists simply sidestep the puzzling perception that suffering is somehow immoral altogether. In his rush to denounce Christianity, Dawkins often portrays the natural world as if it were a vast machine with no moral implications of any kind, and he suggests that we should accept it as such. But we don't. Nor does he. We may not be troubled when a hawk swoops down on an unsuspecting mouse or a lion kills a zebra, but many of us react differently to the ichneumon wasp or a cat that is taunting a mouse that it will soon kill.

Other materialist thinkers have partially explained the perception of immorality that I have been describing. Steven Pinker (drawing on work by Peter Singer and by evolutionary psychologists) has written in detail about the nature of human empathy, speculating that it was evolutionarily adaptive for early humans to empathize with members of their group. Empathy may explain Voltaire's reaction to the Lisbon earthquake, which killed many men and women who were not so different from Voltaire himself. But it is not quite so clear why we are sympathetic to the mouse whose suffering is being prolonged by a cat, and it's even less clear with the caterpillar.

A materialist friend of mine speculates that these examples of natural rapacity may offend a sense of fairness that we have, but he acknowledges that he does not know why such an instinct would be triggered by nonhuman suffering.

Our own suffering raises an additional puzzle. Why do so many of us react with anger or bitterness when we are afflicted, given that our prospects for survival might be higher if we accepted suffering as part of the natural order? Perhaps the earliest humans often responded with acceptance and resolve, but the tendency to moralize suffering does not seem new. Although the Stoics counseled their followers to greet hardship and suffering with acceptance, for instance, they acknowledged our impulse to recoil against suffering and its indignities. "If the ills of the body afflict you," Marcus Aurelius reminded himself and his readers, "reflect that the mind has but to detach itself and apprehend its own powers, to be no longer involved with the movements of the flesh."[6]

The vast array of experiments being conducted by evolutionary psychologists may provide increasingly interesting insights into these questions. The important point here is that we experience many kinds of suffering as immoral, rather than simply accepting them as part of the natural order. The perception of immorality is starkly at odds with the suggestion that the processes of nature are amoral, and it is not yet fully explained even by the most nuanced materialist accounts based on unguided evolution.

Our perception that suffering is wrong certainly does not prove that Christianity can explain suffering whereas materialism cannot. The perception does not tell us anything about why suffering exists in the first place. But it suggests that our experience of suffering is profoundly puzzling, even for materialists.

A Shortcut?

If Christians could show that disasters or illnesses are no coincidence, perhaps this would tip the balance in favor of a Christian understanding of suffering and evil. Although a residue of mystery would remain—the vexing question of why evil exists— our ability to glean the meaning of awful events would show that even apparently random suffering like the Lisbon earthquake is not random at all.

Christians have often been tempted by this solution to the problem of suffering. In the 1980s, some Christians interpreted the AIDS epidemic as God's punishment of homosexuals. Because many of those afflicted by AIDS had embraced a sexually promiscuous lifestyle, the reasoning went, God was punishing them for their immorality. After a tsunami devastated Asia in 2004, a few Christians pointed out that the area hit by the storm was a region with a tiny Christian population and that the region had often been hostile to Christianity.

As materialists have pointed out, and many Christians have agreed, these claims to divine the meaning of awful disasters raise questions that are at least as disturbing as the ones they purport to answer. Why would God allow a tsunami to kill many innocent children, even if some of those killed were hostile to Christianity?

Are Christian prayers that one coastline be spared by a hurricane answered if the hurricane devastates another coastline instead?

Even if it were possible to assign meaning to particular instances of suffering more persuasively than we can, there would be very good reasons to hesitate to do so. If all pains were penalties—if every harm were richly deserved—people would be even more heartless than we already are. Why sympathize? After all, the victims got what they deserved.

This is not what Christianity teaches at all, of course. The irony of Christians' efforts to attach meaning to suffering is that they make Christianity's explanation of suffering seem far less compelling than it actually is. The world is more disorderly and more cripplingly unpredictable than we like to believe. On this one point, a more compelling Christian conception of suffering is not so different, oddly enough, from the perspective of a materialist like Christopher Hitchens, the contrarian public intellectual and author of *God Is Not Great: How Religion Ruins Everything*.

Two Firsthand Accounts of Suffering

In June 2010, Hitchens woke up in a New York City hotel room in excruciating pain, "feeling," as he put it in *Mortality*, his last book, "as if I was actually shackled to my own corpse." He managed to appear on *The Daily Show* with Jon Stewart and at an event with the author Salman Rushdie the same day, though he "did vomit two times . . . just before each show," because of what tests would soon identify as esophageal cancer.[7]

Both Bill Stuntz—who had been chronicling his cancer treatments on a blog we coauthored for two years by the time of Hitchens's diagnosis—and Hitchens retained a dark but characteristic sense of humor throughout their ordeals. "How happily I measured off my day as I saw the injection [of painkiller] being readied," Hitchens wrote, "like the sad goons who raid pharmacies for Oxy-Contin."[8] Speaking of his painkillers and other medications, Stuntz wrote, "When I travel, I'm a walking pharmacy. My coat pockets have a street value."[9]

Hitchens and Stuntz also both emphasized the importance of living as fully as possible even as their cancers worsened. "During this time of what he called 'living dyingly,'" Hitchens's wife wrote in an afterword to *Mortality*, "he insisted ferociously on living, and his constitution, physical and philosophical, did all it could do to stay alive."[10] For Stuntz, living with cancer was "living weak," a slogan he found more apt than the call for cancer patients to "live strong." "There is something inexpressibly lovely," he wrote, "about ordinary tasks done for love of the tasks, and done while in the grip of a disease that seems determined to make those tasks impossible."[11]

If Stuntz had lived longer or Hitchens had gotten his cancer diagnosis a year earlier, someone might well have asked them to have a public conversation about their respective ordeals. Although Hitchens was more famous, Stuntz was the leading criminal justice scholar of his generation and one of America's best-known Christian intellectuals. I'm not sure whether Stuntz would have agreed to appear on the same stage. Whereas Hitchens rarely turned down an opportunity to joust—"debating and lecturing are part of the breath of life to me," as he put it[12]—Stuntz disliked point-counterpoint debates. He nearly backed out of a public conversation with Richard John Neuhaus, the late editor of *First Things*, at the end of both of their lives, when he began to suspect it could turn into a debate. But perhaps he would have given in, at least if the format were sufficiently controlled.

I often imagine how the conversation would have gone, with Hitchens leaning back in a chair as he often did and Stuntz occasionally standing up and supporting himself with a cane. Two of the most revealing questions would be these: Did their suffering have a purpose? And, is suffering immoral?

The first question is quite easy for a materialist like Hitchens to answer. "To the dumb question 'Why me?'" he wrote, "the cosmos barely bothers to return the reply: Why not?" Hitchens acknowledged that, as a heavy smoker who consumed a quart of liquor a day at times, he had been smitten by "exactly the cancer that my age and former 'lifestyle' would suggest I got." But he didn't think he either deserved or didn't deserve the cancer. Many infants get cancer, he pointed out, and many who live unhealthy lives do not. Getting cancer or not is simply a fact of life.[13]

Hitchens's answer to the second question—whether suffering is immoral—probably would not have been quite as straightforward. In his writings, he distinguished suffering and death inflicted by one group on another from suffering that is part of the natural order. In *God Is Not Great*, he chronicled the religious violence he saw in his years as a reporter. "Just to stay within the letter 'B,'" he wrote, he had witnessed appalling "religiously inspired cruelty" in Belfast, Bombay, Belgrade, Bethlehem and Baghdad.[14] Hitchens was not a pacifist—he famously and controversially defended America's war with Iraq—but he excoriated violence he believed to be motivated by religious or political disputes. For Hitchens, the suffering inflicted in these contexts is deeply immoral.

Some might question whether a materialist like Hitchens had an objective basis for calling some behavior acceptable and some evil, since he believed we are the products of an impersonal universe. But whatever the ultimate basis for his moral commitments, there is no doubt they were fervently held. Much more than the other outspoken New Atheists—Richard Dawkins, Daniel Dennett and Sam Harris—Hitchens was a passionate moralist.

Hitchens's moralism did not extend to his cancer or to the suffering that is an inevitable feature of the natural world. He insisted that his cancer had no moral significance. Yet he seemed unable to resist the language of morality altogether. He refers to the "malice" of his cancer in *Mortality*, before catching himself and saying, "There I go again." He also refers to the cancer as an "alien" that "had colonized a bit of my lung" and brought "spreading dead-zone colonies."[15]

For Stuntz, this second question was much easier to answer than the first. Unlike Hitchens, he believed that his cancer and other forms of suffering are genuinely wrong—evidence that the world has been corrupted—just as suffering inflicted by humans is. Speaking of the constant pain in his back, Stuntz wrote that the "sense that my back was not made—that *I* was not made—to feel like *this* is so real and hard that I sometimes think I can touch it, grasp it." Sometimes he wished he didn't believe "that a world exists in which backs like mine don't hurt." "To me," he wrote, it is "akin to being told there is a pill or a surgery that would leave me utterly pain-free—but that I may not have it, and I will not be told why."[16]

Stuntz's answer to the first question—whether he deserved cancer and chronic pain—was more complex. On the narrow question of deserving cancer, his answer was similar to Hitchens's. "Though I deserve every bad thing that ever happened to me," Stuntz wrote, "those things didn't happen *because* I deserve them."[17] Stuntz's understanding of the larger question of whether suffering always has a purpose shifted over the eleven years of his health ordeals. "Our Father's ordering of events is so often hard to swallow," Stuntz wrote in a private email shortly after his back problems began, "and yet so vastly superior to our plans." This view, and this way of stating it, is held by many Christians. God arranges suffering for particular purposes, the reasoning goes, such as disciplining the person who suffers or building their character.

Stuntz later came to a very different view. "God does indeed discipline his children," he wrote. "But not all pains are penalties; life is much less orderly than that."[18] He believed that God does not ordain suffering. From our human perspective, suffering is often meaningless. But it is never pointless. God sometimes allows it and then uses its awfulness to produce something good. Stuntz often illustrated this conclusion with the story of Joseph in the book of Genesis. After Joseph's brothers sold him into slavery, Joseph ended up in Egypt, where he was falsely accused of attempted rape, but eventually rose to prominence and was able to save his family and those around them from famine. "That doesn't mean that slavery and unjust imprisonment *are* good," Stuntz wrote. "Rather, the point is that they *produced* good, and the good they produced was larger than the wickedness that was visited upon Joseph."[19]

The difference between saying that God causes suffering, as many Christians do, and saying that God allows and eventually transforms suffering, may seem merely semantic. But I don't think it is, and Stuntz certainly didn't. He called "the principle of taking the sourest lemons and making the sweetest lemonade . . . the most beautiful idea I've ever encountered."[20]

Varieties of Suffering

Although the suffering occasioned by disease is often the most awful of the many forms of human suffering, there are many others, of course. In a recent book on suffering, Timothy Keller speaks of the suffering of betrayal, suffering of loss and suffering we bring on ourselves, among others.[21] Nearly all of us face suffering of varying magnitudes as a result of strained or broken relationships. One of my own most vivid childhood memories is walking back with a friend from the friend's house when I was twelve and seeing a huge moving van in front of our house as we turned the corner onto my street. Only after a moment's reflection did I realize that the movers had come to pick up my father's belongings, because my parents were divorcing. The sources of some forms of suffering are easier to discern than that of a terrible disease, but many of the emotions we experience are similar.

Ugliness and Embrace

We mustn't downplay the sheer ugliness of suffering and its affront to the dignity of the sufferer. Neither Hitchens nor Stuntz did. Hitchens described the "switch from chronic constipation to its sudden dramatic opposite; the equally nasty double cross of feeling acute hunger while fearing even the scent of food; the absolute misery of gut-wringing nausea on an empty stomach."[22] Stuntz wrote, "Since the surgery to remove the tumor, my gut hurts worse than either [my back or my leg]. And I cannot shake the sense of ugliness. It clings to me, like a stain that cannot be cleansed. My friends and family members may not see the worst of it, but I see—and even I'm repulsed."[23]

We in the West try to deny the ugliness of suffering—just as we try to deny death. In nineteenth-century America, suffering and death were a normal part of life. This is one reason death and personifications of death figure so prominently in Emily Dickinson's poetry. ("Because I could not stop for death— / He kindly stopped for me.")[24] In our era, we export suffering to hospitals, where it is hidden from those who are healthy. According to one recent estimate, roughly 80 percent of all deaths in America take place in a hospital or nursing home.[25] But the separation of the healthy from the unwell does not diminish the ugliness and indignity of suffering; it often makes it worse for those who are suffering.

In the Bible, the ugliness and indignity of suffering show up in a very surprising place—in one of the most glorious Old Testament prophesies of the coming of a Savior. Speaking of the promised redeemer, who would be "high and lifted up," the prophet Isaiah wrote that "his appearance was so marred, beyond human semblance," that "he had no form or majesty that we should look at him, / and no beauty that we should desire him," and that "we esteemed him stricken, smitten by God, and afflicted" (Isaiah 52:14; 53:2, 4). Jesus as depicted here bears very little resemblance to the blond-haired, blue-eyed paintings of him that adorned millions of kitchen and living room walls in twentieth-century America.

The Jesus who was beaten and crucified was indeed marred "beyond human semblance." His suffering was not just physical; it also was psychological. His closest friends abandoned him during his suffering; the apostle Peter pointedly denied knowing Jesus as he waited in the courtyard during Jesus' first trial. At the moment of Jesus' death, he was separated even from God, to whom he cried out, "My God, my God, why have you forsaken me?" (Mark 15:34). Keller has described the utter isolation of this moment as "cosmic abandonment."[26]

The fact that the Son of God suffered an ignominious death means that God fully understands suffering. Although the Bible doesn't explain why suffering exists, it teaches that the Son of God—the second of God's three persons—has experienced suffering firsthand. Pain and suffering are still ugly, but Jesus' having suffered put the ordeal of suffering in a different light.

Let me make the same point in a somewhat different way. When skeptics of Christianity point to the problem of evil, they usually suggest that, if suffering exists, there cannot be a good God. But their reasoning also implies that, if God does exist, he should be punished for permitting this suffering. Christians certainly do not believe that God deserved to be punished. But if he did, he was. God did not simply allow suffering and walk away from it. Jesus took this responsibility on himself, and died on our behalf. Abandoned by every one of his friends—and even temporarily by God himself—and thus utterly alone, he hung on a wooden cross, the shameful death Rome inflicted on the most detestable criminals.

The Bible teaches one other thing about suffering as well. Not only does God understand suffering and not only has he experienced suffering, but he embraces us in our suffering. This is the key message in the book of Job. When everything Job has is destroyed, and he is afflicted with diseases that make him loathsome to behold, his friends—"Job's comforters"—offer plausible-sounding theological explanations for his suffering. Job rejects all their explanations, and in the end he, not the comforters, is the one who is vindicated. God responds just as Job had predicted in the midst of his suffering: "You will call and I will answer you; / you will long for the creature your hands have made" (Job 14:15 NIV).

Christianity teaches that God does indeed long for us in our suffering, that God experienced it personally in Jesus' death and that our deep sense that suffering is immoral—that it is wrong—is not mistaken. This does not answer every question we may have about suffering. But it does seem to me to explain some of the most puzzling features of suffering as we experience it in our own lives.

During the course of his ordeal, my friend Bill Stuntz adopted Job's story as his own. (So much so that a former student drew a lovely picture based on Job 14:15-16 to give to him as a gift, and the *New York Times* quoted from these verses in his obituary.)[27] "God longs for relationship with Job, and Job knows it," Stuntz wrote near the end of his life. "God is the Lover who will not rest until his arms enfold the beloved. . . . So I have found in the midst of pain and heartache and cancer."[28]

4

THE JUSTICE PARADOX

T. S. Eliot once wrote that great poets teach *"what it feels like* to hold certain beliefs."[1] For instance, he says Dante's *Inferno* transports us into the world of medieval Catholicism; we begin to sense what it would mean to embrace this understanding of reality. Eliot contends that certain poetic works do more than simply describe a set of ideas; they bring the implications of these ideas to life. Although they are rarely confused with great poetry, legal systems do the same thing. Legal systems tell us a great deal about how those who crafted them understand the world to work—especially their vision of justice.

The implications are easiest to see in nations whose legal systems have sprung directly from a set of ideas, as with Mosaic law in ancient Israel or the Napoleonic Code in early nineteenth-century France. In other contexts, the links between ideas and actual laws may be a little harder to trace out. Much of America's legal system was borrowed from England, for instance, but the ideas that animate American law differ dramatically from England's and began to diverge very early in America's history. Similarly, although Japanese law was remade in an American image after World War II, it quickly evolved to reflect Japanese ideas rather than American ones.

There is nothing especially surprising about this, once you start to think about it. Nearly every system of thought gives rise to a theory of justice. If the proof is in the pudding, a nation's or civilization's legal system is the pudding. The legal system and its effects show us the real-world implications of the system of thought that underlies it.

It is here that a more surprising reality enters in. Whether it's an ancient judicial system, Roman law, the Napoleonic Code or a libertarian system inspired by the ideas of nineteenth-century British philosopher John Stuart Mill, its advocates invariably seem to persuade themselves that the right laws can produce a just moral order.

In the prologue to one of the earliest known legal codes, Hammurabi wrote that "the god Marduk commanded me to provide just ways for the people of the land [to attain] appropriate behavior," and he vowed that his laws would "[establish] truth and justice as the declaration of the land." How would he do this? One portion of Hammurabi's Code instructed that a judge who got a decision wrong must not only be fined; he also must be permanently removed from his position. (I sometimes wonder what our own systems of justice would look like if we adopted a rule like this!) Our evidence about the ancient Near East is sketchy, but it is highly unlikely that Hammurabi's Code fulfilled its promise.

Rulers, philosophers and their followers have continued to make similar promises ever since, yet the legal codes have never succeeded in producing a just social order. Both parts of the pattern— the hubris about our capacity for justice and the failure that follows—are important. It would be one thing if we knew that our legal systems would inevitably fail and did our best in the face of this reality. But we don't. The men and women who devise them inevitably think they will work.

This paradox—the justice paradox—is perhaps the least familiar of the paradoxes I have explored in this book, but it is in some respects the most revealing of all. It may be useful to start with several modern examples. The first is obvious; the second a little more subtle.

Marxism as an Example

The most obvious illustration of heady dreams for a just social order that never materialized in the past century was Marxism. The source of a newly just social order, according to Marx, would be a revolutionary shift to working-class control—a dictatorship of the proletariat—that would resolve the conflict between labor and capital. The Marxist ideas that were put into practice after the Russian Revolution in the 1910s departed in some respects from "pure" Marxism, of course, as did the twentieth century's other awful experiments with communist ideas. The followers of Stalin and Trotsky in Russia each thought the other was dangerously misguided, and Mao served up another version of communism altogether. But each group insisted they were creating a new order that would solve the problems of the past. Human greed would be reined in and class distinctions removed. Yet class distinctions did not disappear. They simply took another form, with party insiders replacing aristocracy at the top of the hierarchy. Whatever harmony existed was imposed by often-brutal force, rather than emerging naturally from the men and women of a transformed society.

America's Justice Paradox

Because its claims were so grandiose and its dramatic collapse is still recent, Marxism is almost too obvious an illustration of the justice paradox. To show that the dilemma is pervasive, let's turn to an example that is much closer to home for many of us: the United States.

In some respects, the framers of America's constitutional experiment were more clear-eyed and realistic than the founders of almost any other system. Because James Madison and his colleagues recognized the dangers of factions and the risk that power will be abused, they designed an intricate system of checks and balances. The executive, the legislative and the judicial branches of government each have separate powers and serve as constraints on one another. Before a new law can go into effect, both houses of Congress must vote in favor, and the president must sign it, and even then it is subject to judicial review. These features make the American experiment quite cautious and realistic by historical standards—much more cautious, for instance, than the French Revolution that was taking place at the same time, calling for "*Liberté, Egalité, Fraternité.*"

The appearances are misleading, however. Although the founders recognized the risk that power would be misused, even they sometimes seemed to think that properly crafted laws could fix the problem. The Constitution's Preamble, which speaks on behalf of "We the People," proclaims an intention to "establish justice" and "ensure domestic tranquility." These are rhetorical flourishes, but the optimism in the founding documents about what can be done with law is unmistakable. Nor did this optimism disappear. A century later, after the Civil War ended slavery and the Thirteenth, Fourteenth and Fifteenth Amendments removed its stain from the Constitution, many American leaders thought a truly just society was on the horizon.

The summit of American legal optimism in the modern era came with the enactment of Prohibition in 1919, with the support of a large majority of Americans, and the implementation of its constitutional ban on the manufacture or sale of alcohol the following year. We now tend to view Prohibition as a quixotic campaign that is highly unlikely ever to be repeated. This may be true in a narrow sense—it's hard to imagine a movement to remove alcohol from American households and bars getting off the ground. But in a broader sense, the spirit of Prohibition lives on. Americans' confidence in the curative powers of the law has not dimmed a whit. Lawmakers continue to pass laws designed to regulate morality, such as the laws making many forms of gambling (most recently, Internet gambling) illegal, and other laws creating a special category of additional punishment for hate crimes. Americans may gripe that the Supreme Court has "abandoned the Constitution" or no longer honors the rule of law, but they have considerable faith that society can be perfected with the right legal code. Americans, too, are susceptible to the justice paradox.

I do not mean to suggest that every system of justice is equally flawed. The US system is remarkably good by historical standards. In much of the world, rapes go unpunished, especially if the rapist is well connected or willing to pay a small bribe. Not so in the United States. But serious shortcomings remain. Large numbers of innocent defendants are convicted each year; at current rates of incarceration, 33 percent of all black men who do not have a college education and 60 percent of all who drop out of high school will spend time in prison.[2] There are better and worse systems of justice—some might put Denmark or Sweden at the top—but poke around a little, and it turns out that even the best has major flaws.

A Pantheist or Dualist Explanation

Does any religion or system of thought provide a plausible explanation of the justice paradox?

Pantheism comes closer than most other religious alternatives. If supernatural forces pervade the universe, as pantheists believe, good and evil will be common features of our experience and the coexistence of the two would seem to be permanent. At the least, there is no reason to believe that human beings can create a social order that will keep evil entirely at bay, since it is part of the fabric of the universe. We shouldn't expect any permanent solution to evil in pantheism: if evil can never be eradicated, human systems of justice will always be precarious and incomplete.

Pantheism's chief shortcoming in this context is that it provides a very good explanation of the second part of the justice paradox—our inability to achieve justice—but gives little insight into the first—the repeated optimism throughout human history that this time is different, that some new theory of justice will succeed where all of its predecessors have failed. Pantheistic perspectives suggest that the optimists are deluded, but they don't explain why the optimism is so ubiquitous a feature of human history.

Dualist accounts that draw a sharp distinction between spirit and matter are problematic for different reasons. Gnosticism is one flavor of dualism that finds matter to be evil and encourages us to flee from it. Somewhat like pantheism, it helps us understand why injustice exists, but gives us no reason to expect—or motivation to work toward—a just social order. Why, if matter is evil, would we ever be fooled by the illusion that the right legal code can give us a just social order?

Likewise, dualists of a deist inclination—that is, those who believe that God or the gods are far removed from human affairs—give us few resources for understanding why the justice paradox is so ubiquitous. Deists have tended to believe that justice is possible, perhaps because humans need not worry about interference from supernatural forces and can place their confidence squarely in human capacity. Evidence of this perspective can be seen in the deist influence on the American Constitution and its optimism in the capacity of human reason to establish justice. Yet the historical evidence suggests that we are unlikely to achieve a just social order through law. A deist view of the world is confounded by both halves of the justice paradox.

A Materialist Explanation?

The best-known contemporary, nonreligious theories of justice are John Stuart Mill's utilitarianism and the more recent theory of justice advocated by John Rawls.[3] Although utilitarianism comes in a variety of different flavors (there are distinctions between act-based and rule-based, and between hedonistic and preference-based), it focuses on, as the cliché has it, promoting the greatest good for the greatest number. Under Rawls's theory of justice, a society should start with a minimum level of protection for the least well-off and should permit laws that lead to inequalities in society only if the inequality benefits the least well-off.

By themselves, these theories give us ways of thinking about justice, but do not necessarily speak to the question of whether it's possible to achieve a truly just society. Unlike Marx, neither Mill nor Rawls claimed that his vision of justice was inevitable. Advocates of these theories inevitably do take positions on the justice question, however. Several prominent contemporary materialists have done just this, incorporating utilitarian perspectives into their writings on issues related to justice. Their insights offer a stark challenge to nearly everything I have said thus far about the justice paradox.

The key to understanding the materialist perspective lies in two features of many materialists' understanding of human beings and our place in the world that seem contradictory at first. The first is that humans do not belong on a pedestal. We are not special, belonging in a separate category from animals and other forms of life on Earth. The second is that, in principle, we and our institutions are perfectible.

Start with the materialist perspective on what it means to be human. Many materialists insist that the traditional understanding that human beings are superior to other animals, as reflected in the hierarchical chain-of-being diagrams that were popular at the outset of the scientific revolution, is mistaken. A materialist friend of mine likes to say that if he were forced to pick one life form as superior, he would probably pick insects or bacteria. Both have colonized the world far more than humans ever will, and if a massive meteor were to destroy the earth as we know it, insects and bacteria would be the life forms most likely to survive. Rather than a hierarchy with human beings on top, the preferred metaphor for many materialists is a vast and intricately branched tree or a web, reflecting the view that all current life evolved from the same ancestral forms.

If men and women are not special—if we were created a little lower than the ants—this might seem to suggest that the prospects for human justice are dim. But materialism doesn't require materialists to draw such a conclusion. While there is no guarantee that any given human society or human society as a whole will improve, materialism doesn't rule out the possibility that it will. To be sure, evolution has disposed us to favor our family or clan. But these instincts are only that, instincts; they are not imperatives. We can resist them. Richard Dawkins has made precisely this point in characteristically eloquent prose: "We have the power to defy the selfish genes of our birth and, if necessary, the selfish genes of our indoctrination. We can even discuss ways of deliberately cultivating and nurturing pure, disinterested altruism—something that has no place in nature, something that has never existed before in the whole history of the world."[4]

Materialists have been highly critical of the moral codes and legal systems of the past. But their objections are generally based on a rejection of the supernatural authority on which most of these moral codes have been based. When a New Atheist ridicules the rules in the Mosaic law that were designed to distinguish Israel from the nations around it—such as the prohibition against eating shrimp and other shellfish—or when he dismisses the Jewish and Muslim prohibition against eating pork as an irrational taboo, his target is religious belief, not the possibility of establishing a just social order.

Indeed, some materialists believe that by undermining belief in the supernatural, materialism can pave the way for a just social order. "The facts of science," Steven Pinker, the Harvard linguist, writes, "by exposing the absence of purpose in the law governing the universe, force us to take responsibility for the welfare of ourselves, our species, and our planet."[5] In his influential book *The Better Angels of Our Nature*, Pinker provides the historical context for this claim and his optimism about its implications. He argues that the combination of modern governments (which came with the emergence of nation-states five hundred years ago) and international trade, together with the Enlightenment ideals of John Locke, David Hume and others, has enabled us to rein in our violent tendencies. Pinker points to the sea change in the rights of women, blacks, gays and animals over the past century as part of this turn from violence, arguing that violence against each has declined. These developments also are evidence, he suggests, that justice is increasing in human society. As the materialist friend I mentioned earlier put it in an email message, referring to Pinker's book, "We have good reason to be optimistic about society and the progress towards a just social order."

Perhaps we are indeed capable of achieving a truly just society, and the justice paradox will prove to be illusory. But the evidence is shaky. Pinker's principal claim—which is a claim about violence and only indirectly about justice—is quite compelling and backed by mountains of painstakingly surveyed statistical evidence. But even here Pinker seems to me to overstate recent trends, such as the Long Peace since the end of World War II, in several key respects. He relies heavily on tendencies in developed Western democracies

and seems to assume that democracy and the Enlightenment rationality that characterizes European and American democracy will
take hold throughout the world. Yet it is not at all clear that this is
the case.

In an imaginary graduation speech at the outset of the book,
Pinker describes, among other things, the decline in hostilities in
the Middle East in the decades since his own graduation from
college. But in the three years since the publication of *The Better
Angels of Our Nature* in 2011, with its imaginary graduation speech,
we have seen the collapse of democracy in Egypt and a horrific civil
war in Syria. The Middle East no longer looks quite as peaceful.
The pervasive violence in parts of Africa and Latin America lie
outside Pinker's focus on the contemporary West. Although he
does not ignore them, they are given short shrift in his analysis.

Pinker's hints that society is becoming more peaceful depend
heavily on an assumption that the ability of a stable state to control
violence, together with increased equality, will translate to increasingly just societies around the world. But the stable state in Pinker's
story is a black box, a benign Leviathan whose only role is providing justice and peace. If we look inside the black box, the state
and its contributions to justice are messier than Pinker lets on. It
is true, as Pinker claims, that far fewer blacks are murdered on
racial grounds in the United States than a century ago, but it is also
true that "a term in the local penitentiary has become an ordinary
life experience" for black males, as one scholar puts it.[6] For lower-
and lower-middle-class Americans, both white and black, the
family has collapsed, with large majorities of children born in
single-parent homes. Even America, the richest nation in the

world, is a far cry from achieving a truly just society. If we look beyond America and the wealthier European nations, the departures from justice are far greater. In many developing nations, the wealthy are able to purchase safety for themselves, but the poor are surrounded by violence.

The Temptation to Take a Shortcut

Even if materialists were right about the perfectibility of human justice, which seems extremely unlikely, their optimism carries a very serious potential cost. The belief that we can achieve a just social order can create a dangerous temptation to speed up the process of getting there. In the early decades of Darwinism, this temptation gave rise to the eugenics movement, one of whose chief early proponents was Darwin's cousin Francis Galton. Inspired by natural selection, advocates of eugenics believed that social elites could take selection into their own hands and perfect society by preventing mentally or physically inferior citizens from reproducing. These views, which later contributed to some of the horrid atrocities of Nazi Germany, reflected a radical misunderstanding of natural selection and Darwinism.

Pinker himself is at pains to distance the trends he extols from eugenics. Although Darwinism and Enlightenment reasoning shaped many of the early advocates of eugenics, Pinker insists the atrocities of eugenics were caused not by these factors, but by Romantic nationalism and mythical beliefs about the destiny of the German people. I think Pinker has a point, at least about the winds that turned the evil early sparks into a bonfire. And I want to be clear that current materialists do not hold views remotely like those of the eugenicists. But it also seems undeniable that, if our theory of reality holds that human society may be perfectible, there will be a strong temptation to take shortcuts to achieve that perfection.

Those who are optimistic about justice also may be tempted to impose restrictions on views that strike them as unenlightened. Pinker worries, for instance, that advocates of traditional values and religious perspectives could interfere with the onward march of progress, due to their "loathing of modernity" and "long[ing] to turn back the clock."[7] Materialists who share this distaste for religion may place a low value on religious freedom, especially when it seems to conflict with rights of groups that materialists are more inclined to protect.

This does not mean that optimism about the human capacity to achieve justice will inevitably overstep its bounds in these ways. But it could, and we need to be wary of the temptations.

The Christian Story

Unlike materialism, Christianity insists humans and human society are not perfectible, even in principle. Christians believe that we are incapable of producing a truly just society and that the legal codes we create to foster morality will always fail. The dream of a perfectly just social order is, Christians believe, a dangerous lie that we tell ourselves. If human beings are capable of achieving perfect justice, Christianity is mistaken. But if we are not, it is materialism and other systems of thought that may be mistaken.

The other monotheistic religions also raise questions about our perfectibility. The Old Testament story of Adam and Eve, which is accepted by Muslims as well as Jews, teaches that our earliest parents violated the prohibition against eating from the tree of the knowledge of good and evil because they thought that eating the fruit would make them equal to God. The Tower of Babel recounts another effort to achieve parity with God—this time by building a spectacular tower that reached toward the heavens. The theme of human hubris about our capacity to control our destiny runs through the entire Old Testament.

But Christianity goes further. Not only does it teach that every one of us is a lawbreaker when it comes to the moral law, but Christianity, unlike any other major religion or system of thought, rests on a story in which law fails.

Before I illustrate these points from the New Testament accounts of Jesus' arrest, trial and execution, let me emphasize that you do not need to place any particular confidence in the historical accuracy of the New Testament to appreciate how radically different Christianity is from any other religion or system of thought. Perhaps you suspect that the story was altered long after Jesus' life and death, and that many of the details are subject to question. I hope you will one day be persuaded that the accounts can be trusted, but that is not my concern here. My concern is to show that Christianity is a story about how even the very best human laws will inevitably fail. Whether the story is truth, fiction or some combination of the two, there is no doubt whatsoever about the message it is intended to convey.

In Jesus' final days, he came face-to-face with two different legal systems.[8] His encounters with ancient justice began when Judas, one of his twelve apostles, led representatives of Israel's religious authorities to the hideaway where Jesus had gone after eating Passover dinner. Once Jesus had been apprehended, the religious leaders immediately brought him to trial. The Jewish law that governed Jesus' trial came from the legal rules set forth in the Old Testament, known as the Mosaic law, together with additional rules developed over the centuries for its implementation. Fastidious in their protection of vulnerable defendants, these laws gave defendants a full trial and required that charges be substantiated by the testimony of two witnesses.

The most striking feature of Jesus' trial is how well the protections seemed to work, at least at first. Although the religious leaders wanted to remove the threat that Jesus posed to their authority, they struggled to find two witnesses who could testify to his having committed a crime punishable by death. "Many testified falsely against him," the Bible says, "but their statements did not agree" (Mark 14:56 NIV).

The impasse was broken only after the high priest interjected himself into the proceedings and asked Jesus, "Are you the Christ, the Son of the Blessed?" (Mark 14:61). When Jesus stated that he was indeed both Christ and the Son of God, the high priest immediately ended the trial, declaring Jesus guilty of blasphemy for having equated himself with God. The high priest's intervention was illegal, because he was forbidden by Jewish law from participating in a capital trial prior to the vote on the verdict. So too were other aspects of the trial (including its being conducted at night, without formal charges or the opportunity for a defense). But the religious leaders now had a basis for declaring Jesus guilty.

Because Rome did not permit Israel's religious leaders to carry out a capital punishment, they asked Pontius Pilate, the local Roman ruler, to sentence Jesus to death. This led to a second trial, this time under Roman law. The second trial was an inversion of the first. Unlike the corner-cutting religious leaders, Pilate refused to condemn Jesus unless there were formal charges. This seems to have stymied the religious leaders, apparently because they doubted that Pilate would put Jesus to death for blasphemy. If Pilate wasn't willing to execute Jesus simply to keep the religious leaders happy, he probably wasn't going to be persuaded that a religious dispute between a Jew and the Jewish leaders that had very little to do with Pilate or his office was a good reason to execute Jesus.

Jesus' accusers scrambled to come up with a more impressive allegation and finally got Pilate's attention by accusing Jesus of treason. Jesus had resisted paying taxes to Rome, they claimed (falsely, since Jesus had expressly instructed his disciples to "give to Caesar what is Caesar's" when asked about taxes; Mark 12:17), and he had proclaimed himself to be "Christ, a king" (Luke 23:2). Jesus, they insisted, had thumbed his nose at Pilate and Rome.

Pilate's reaction once again inverted the earlier trial. Unlike the religious leaders, who saw the legal process as a way to have Jesus put to death, Pilate sensed that Jesus was innocent and tried to use the legal process to set him free. Pilate saw legal technicalities as a way to solve his problem. He tried to dodge the case altogether, first by telling the religious leaders that they should judge Jesus themselves and then by turning Jesus over to Herod, the ruler of Galilee, when Pilate learned that Jesus came from Galilee.

Neither ploy worked. The religious leaders demanded an execution, which only a Roman official could authorize, and Herod handed Jesus right back to Pilate. So Pilate tried to persuade Jesus to mount a defense. In Pilate's court, corners would not be cut.

Even after Jesus declined to defend himself, Pilate did not immediately order his execution. Pilate invoked his own precedent of letting one condemned prisoner go free during Passover. He gave the crowd that had gathered to watch the coming crucifixions a choice, expecting them to choose Jesus, but the crowd chose an insurrectionist named Barabbas instead. Pilate insisted that "I find no basis for a charge against him" (John 18:38 NIV), but in the end he handed Jesus over to be crucified.

What do we learn from the two trials? The laws that governed the first trial were based on the same laws that Jesus himself said he came not to abolish but to fulfill (Matthew 5:17). It wasn't simply that the Jewish religious law failed to protect Jesus as it was intended to do. The law's effect was much worse than this. It legitimized actions that otherwise would have been recognized as illegitimate. Imagine what would have happened if the religious leaders had simply killed Jesus without going through the charade of a trial, as the New Testament suggests they were tempted to do at other points in his public ministry. An assassination would have revealed their actions for what they were and would have put the leaders at risk of a populist backlash. They might even have been tried for murder. By bringing Jesus to trial, they avoided these problems. The legal system legitimized their injustice.

The second trial should have cured the defects of the first. Pilate did not have any animus against Jesus, and he was convinced that Jesus was innocent of the charge of having refused to pay taxes to Caesar. Yet, once again, the law failed. Although the Roman legal system gave Pilate an array of possible escape hatches to avoid condemning an innocent man, none of them worked.

The Jewish and Roman legal systems were not unusually bad—
especially by ancient legal standards. These were two of the finest
legal systems the world had ever known, and this is precisely the
point. The hero of the Christian story was murdered by impressive
legal systems, not transparently evil ones. Lest we think that it is
simply an accident that one system of law failed, the Jesus story
shows that even two legal systems working together and poten-
tially correcting one another cannot ensure a just outcome. The
justice paradox lies at the very heart of the Christian story.

It is possible that the past is not prologue when it comes to
justice. Perhaps the failure of every legal system humans have ever
established in the past does not mean we are incapable of achieving
a fully just social order. But it seems much more likely that the
justice paradox is indeed a true paradox. If it is, Christianity provides a more plausible explanation than any other religion or
system of thought of where our misplaced belief in law's power
comes from and where it can lead.

Christianity's Take on the Justice Paradox

If perfect justice is not possible, what does a more realistic vision
of justice look like?

The starting point for a Christian understanding of justice is the
biblical principle that each of us—whatever our race, gender, or
physical and mental firmities or infirmities—is made in the image
of God. There is no Jew or Gentile, no male or female, as the
apostle Paul says (Galatians 3:28). The belief that each one of us is
made in the image of God has been the inspiration for numerous
human rights initiatives throughout history, including the efforts

of the Earl of Shaftsbury to improve the conditions of England's poor in the eighteenth century and William Wilberforce's eventually successful quest to end England's slave trade in the nineteenth. In the twentieth century, this Christian belief served as the foundation for the United Nations Declaration on Human Rights, which was released in 1948 and is rightly seen as the start of the international human rights movement (although religious language was carefully omitted from it).

Christians sometimes argue that human rights are not possible apart from the biblical understanding that we are made in the image of God. This is not quite right. Many materialists believe deeply in human dignity and are firmly committed to human rights, as are many adherents of other religions and systems of thought. The principal difference is the foundation of these beliefs. Materialists often point to some of the trappings of consciousness—such as our ability to make choices about the kind of life we live—as the basis for human dignity. Christians believe that these capacities are not the ultimate basis for human dignity. Our dignity comes from being loved by the God who created the universe. One implication of the distinction is that the materialist conception of dignity seems to suggest that those who are more intelligent or better able to make choices are more valuable than those who are not, while the Christian conception insists that we all have the same dignity, since we are equally loved by God.

The Christian understanding of dignity has another important characteristic as well. If each of us is made in the image of God, and God loves each of us, it is not enough for us to simply respect one another. We have an obligation to actively promote the flourishing of others and to seek their welfare.

In my own scholarly writing, I have argued that a legal system needs to account not just for the fact that each of us is made in the image of God, but also for the human tendency to misbehave.[9] The philosopher Thomas Hobbes famously said that if there were no government and no laws, life would be "nasty, brutish and short." When most of us think about our legal system, the need to restrain misbehavior by ordinary citizens is the first thing that comes to mind. But ordinary citizens are not the only ones who are tempted to misbehave. They are not the only ones who are inherently sinful, as the Bible puts it. Lawmakers and law enforcers have the same inclinations. They too are sinful. If the law imposed penalties for every wrong—from "white lies" to murder—police and prosecutors would have complete discretion to decide who should be sent to prison and who should go free, and business regulators could pick their least favorite corporate executive and punish him or her whenever they chose.

The American experience with Prohibition is again a telling example of how things can go amok. The prohibition of making, selling or transporting alcohol—from 1920 until the repeal of the Eighteenth Amendment became effective in 1933—was far too broad for state and federal regulators to enforce fully and systematically. As a result, regulators had considerable discretion, and the discretion invited discrimination. Someone who sold beer to Italian immigrants on the Lower East Side might well end up in prison. If he sold gin to a more elite clientele on the Upper East Side, he was more likely to wind up in an F. Scott Fitzgerald novel. Because this discriminatory enforcement bred contempt for the law, Prohibition helped to erode the very norms against drinking that the law was intended to strengthen.

If everyone, both citizens and those who govern them, is tempted to misbehave, as a Christian understanding of the justice paradox teaches, we should not be surprised that no human legal system has ever produced a just social order. The human desire to control our own destiny and to assume godlike powers for ourselves explains why men and women have repeatedly convinced themselves that the history of failure does not apply to them—that they will be the ones to prove the past wrong. Christianity makes sense of both parts of the justice paradox.

Do Christians believe that every attempt to promote justice is therefore pointless? Not at all. A Christian understanding of the limits of law, combined with our obligation to promote the flourishing of others, can give us a vision of justice I call "law with a light touch."

Granted, some Christians take a nihilist attitude toward justice, writing off the world as corrupt and beyond fixing. And Christians who are more within the mainstream disagree about the extent to which they should rely on, participate in or seek to shape secular justice. But despite the differences on details, most Christians believe that Christianity has a great deal to say about justice. No legal system can produce true justice, and this fact can help us to think about what our legal systems should and should not aspire to.

If all of us are sinful, legal systems must play a double game: restraining the worst wrongs by the citizenry without empowering judges and prosecutors to do wrong themselves. The key to playing that double game well is to limit law's reach. One implication of this, ironically, is that a less ambitious legal system will often be more effective than a more ambitious one. When it comes to justice, less is often more.

One positive example of how this can work is the civil rights movement. In law schools, we talk a lot about the two great laws that were enacted thanks to the movement: the Civil Rights Act of 1964 and the Voting Rights Act of 1965. But, as Bill Stuntz has written, changing the law wasn't Martin Luther King's primary objective.[10] He was trying to change hearts. King fought and eventually died for the right to have relationship with those who refused to have relationship with him. He wasn't trying to put anyone in prison. In fact, he and his fellow protestors went to prison themselves in their quest to create true relationship in our communities. The true heart of the movement was relationship, not law.

The two laws that the civil rights movement did inspire were very unusual. Unlike many moral and social reforms, the Civil Rights Act and the Voting Rights Act were not criminal laws. They were not designed to put offenders in jail or even to impose damages for the wrongs committed against blacks in the past. The objective of the Civil Rights Act was to give us a more integrated workplace, in which blacks and whites can work side by side. The Voting Rights Act of 1965 created the modern law of voting rights, giving us an integrated political community in which blacks and whites can vote side by side. The main reason these laws have been so successful is that they—unlike so many laws—actually help to create relationships in our communities.

If the dignity that comes from our being made in the image of

God requires that we seek one another's flourishing, as Christians believe it does, one positive contribution that laws can sometimes make is to foster relationships in contexts where they otherwise might not occur. The civil rights laws are a vivid example of this.

Let me give another, more prosaic but nevertheless vital illustration. Responding to the recent financial crisis, which required more than a trillion dollars in rescue funding in the United States alone, commentators divided into two categories. Some insisted that the executives of the banks that failed, such as Bear Stearns and Lehman Brothers, were crooks who should have gone to jail and that lawmakers should have enacted even more regulation than the sweeping new financial reforms adopted in the United States and other countries after the crisis. Others insist that the biggest problem with Wall Street is cultural. Only by restoring trust and by replacing greed with character can Wall Street be reformed.

From a law with a light-touch perspective, both critiques miss the mark. As awful as the culture of Wall Street has become, simply calling for business schools to spend more time teaching ethics and for bankers to be more honorable isn't the solution. Bankers have enormous incentives to take risks and to pay themselves huge amounts of money—incentives that are in part created by the regulatory structure itself. I'm reminded of the "perfectionist" cults of the 1800s, such as the Oneida Community in upstate New York. The leaders of the colony insisted they were so pure that men and women could sleep together, naked, without succumbing to sex. But the temptations were too great. Sex won. Greed won on Wall Street in the 2000s for very similar reasons.

Although culture alone isn't enough, law isn't either. Even the most elaborate laws can be circumvented, especially once a crisis has passed and ordinary citizens are no longer paying as close attention to regulators' enforcement of the regulatory framework. Every parent (and kid) is familiar with the problem. Give kids a list of ten things they can't do, and they are sure to do an eleventh thing that isn't on the list.

What can be done? As with the civil rights movement, the most promising solutions are likely to include both moral norms and law. Even after the recent crisis, if a bank gives its executives stock options—that is, the right but not the obligation to buy a share of stock at a particular price—the bank receives much more favorable tax treatment than if the executive is paid with cash. Yet executives who are paid with stock options are rewarded handsomely if the bank takes big risks and its stock rises in value, but they are not punished if the risk taking doesn't pan out. Few bank executives can resist the temptation to roll the dice. Reforming rules like this one, while rehabilitating a culture of character in financial life, can do more good than either a long list of regulatory dos and don'ts or pleas for the denizens of Wall Street to pay no heed to the irresistible temptations all around them.

Are Christians Hypocrites?

When I tell people about Christianity's revolutionary critique of law's power, I often get an immediate objection: don't Christians always try to use law to promote their vision of a perfectly just legal order? My conversation partners often point to the Roman Empire after Constantine and to the more recent culture-wars debate as examples.

There unfortunately is considerable truth in the objection. In the early centuries of the Christian church, the suggestion that Christians should use legal rules to achieve social morality would have been almost unthinkable. But this changed after Constantine converted to Christianity in the fourth century and began to promote Christianity within the Roman Empire. The legacy of Christendom, as the marriage of Christianity and the state later came to be known, was mixed. I am not knowledgeable enough about the history to try to untangle the good from the bad. But there is no doubt that the power brokers of Christendom often were optimistic about the capacity of the law to achieve a Christian moral order.

During the post–Civil War period in the United States, an era I'm more familiar with, many Christian leaders believed that a new moral order could be established through legal reform. Walter Rauschenbusch, a theologian at Rochester Seminary in New York and the leading figure of a movement known as the social gospel, detected at the end of the nineteenth century "a growing perfection in the collective life of humanity, in our laws, in the customs of society."[11] If Prohibition and vice regulation were enacted and the government took control of key industries, he believed, the "growing perfection" could be ensured. America would look increasingly like the kingdom of God that Jesus teaches about in the New Testament. In the current generation, the politically conservative Christians known as the Religious Right have shown a similar love for legal solutions, although with less of the sunny optimism that many of the social gospelers had.

I am the first to admit that Christians' tendency to love the law too much makes Christianity's explanation of the justice dilemma less persuasive than it might be if Christian reformers did not fall into the same traps as the advocates of other theories of life and reality. Some might argue that the tendency is less pronounced in Christianity than with other views. Although most scholars take a dim view of the Christian exercise of power in the Middle Ages, for instance, revisionist sociologists and historians have recently argued that the criticisms are unfounded and that Christian influence produced many of the advances of the modern era.[12] By this reasoning, Christianity does quite well if we grade on a curve—in comparison to other views.

I don't know whether these defenders of Christianity are right or wrong. Either way, I think there is a better explanation for Christians' optimism about the capacity of power: Christians are not exempt from Christianity's explanation of human nature. Christianity teaches that those who acknowledge their sinfulness and identify themselves with Jesus are reconciled with God, but this does not mean that the temptation to make ourselves, rather than God, the measure of reality suddenly disappears. If our commitment to Christianity is genuine, these tendencies should diminish, but they do not simply go away. Some of the most insidious temptations come when we try to remake the world in our own image, thinking the vision we are promoting is God's.

The same point can be put in another way. Although Christians have been responsible for too many abuses, Christianity is uniquely self-correcting. Let me explain what I mean by this. When the advocates of other views of life and reality seek to establish their vision of justice through a legal code, as did Napoleon in the nineteenth century, Marxism in the twentieth and Islam in some countries today, these efforts are often accurate reflections of the ideas themselves. Napoleon and Marx thought and taught that, with the right legal and political framework, they could establish a just moral order.

When Christians seek to usher in the kingdom of God through law, they are denying Christianity's teachings, not promoting them. Nowhere in the biblical accounts of Jesus' life and ministry do we find a scintilla of evidence that the right legal code can create a just society. Jesus repeatedly criticized the legal excesses of his era, and he himself was, as we have seen, wrongly put to death by two seemingly enlightened systems of justice.

Christianity teaches that law can never transform us. Only the reconciliation with God that Jesus made possible through his suffering on our behalf can do that—a reconciliation achieved at precisely the moment when law and legal process most spectacularly failed. But Christianity also teaches that the universe will one day be put to rights, not by us but by God, and (as I will explain more fully in the next chapter) that our contributions to justice are a foreshadowing, and maybe even a tiny but indelible part, of the true justice for which the universe was designed.

5

LIFE AND AFTERLIFE

There is one paradox that Christians need to explain but materialists do not: the Christian belief in heaven. Like the ancient Egyptians and a few other religions today, but unlike materialists and followers of many other religions, Christians believe that our existence includes both a life and an afterlife. This is the paradox of heaven, or as I will sometimes call it, life and afterlife.

Some materialists believe that Christian conceptions of heaven are especially strong evidence that Christianity is not true. I think they are deeply mistaken about this. Several of the most common objections to heaven are based on misunderstandings about what Christianity teaches about heaven. What Christianity actually says may sound a little strange, but it flows directly from our idea-making capacity, our experience of beauty and suffering, and our longing for justice.

Heaven and the Heavens

The first thing to disentangle is the relationship between heaven—that is, an eternal union with God—and the heavens, in the sense of the sun, the moon and the starry host. According to one common perception, which is reflected in every cartoon that depicts God or a new resident of heaven surrounded by fluffy clouds, heaven can be found only in the heavens. Based on this assumption, critics of Christianity sometimes insist that, if the biblical writers were wrong about the nature of the heavens, they must also have been wrong about the existence of heaven.

Here is an example. In *The Christian Delusion*, a trenchant, wide-ranging critique of Christianity, one of the authors singles out Psalm 19 as proof that heaven does not exist. When the psalm states that "the heavens declare the glory of God," and that the sun's "going forth is from the end of the heaven, and his circuit unto the ends of it," the critic says (quoting the King James Version of the Bible), the psalmist obviously thinks that heaven is a solid domain immediately above Earth and that the sun moves from one side of it to the other. We now know that there is no hard layer above Earth. Earth's visible atmosphere gives way to a layer of ozone and eventually to vast distances of space. This proves, the critic concludes, that our world is not "inhabited by heavenly beings above and shades in Sheol below. Instead we live on the thin outer layer of our planet's shifting surface."[1]

There are two problems with this critique and critiques like it. First, the psalmist isn't making a claim about heaven and the nature of heavenly beings. He is describing one feature of the heavens—the sun.

Second, even if the critic's primary objective were to point out the psalmist's ignorance of astronomy, these verses are an odd illustration. The psalm in question happens to be a particularly beautiful one. C. S. Lewis called it "the greatest poem in the Psalter and one of the greatest lyrics in the world."[2] The writer of the psalm (who is identified as David, Israel's greatest king) probably did believe that the sun moves across the sky, and he also may have thought that the heavens were a flat layer on top of the earth. But even school students who read the psalm immediately recognize that it is not intended to provide a map of the heavens. If the psalmist were given a thorough briefing on contemporary astronomy and his misconceptions about space corrected, I doubt he would change a single word of his poem. He was concerned with the beauty of the sun as it appears at various parts of the day and with extolling God as its and his creator.

Several thousand years later, not much has changed. Even today, poems that speak of sunrises and sunsets still far outnumber those that imagine Earth as orbiting around the sun. The first two of a series of recent movies are called *Before Sunrise* and *Before Sunset*, because the sun seems to rise and set even though the earth is the body that is revolving. Even scientists and science writers use these conventions, lest the quest for technical accuracy make a description mind-numbingly confusing. In a recent article describing the puzzling shortening rather than lengthening of days immediately after the winter solstice, the writer begins in the conventional way, noting that he "had been looking forward to earlier sunrises once the winter solstice was past." He does not stop to remind us that the sun actually does not rise; nor would we want him to.[3]

By using the same interpretative flexibility when we interpret the poetry of the Bible, we can avoid the mistake of conflating poetry with a scientific treatise. We also will be more alert to the role beauty plays in our understanding of the world. The psalmist's poetry may not have been descriptively accurate, but it is emotionally compelling: even a reader who believes that the universe is simply an accident can understand what it feels like to see the sun and sky as the handiwork of God.

Is Heaven a Cosmic Bribe?

Although materialists' critique of the biblical writers' cosmology seems to be designed primarily for scoring rhetorical points, another objection to heaven has more bite. According to this argument, the Christian belief in heaven is a form of wish fulfillment. As he so often does, Richard Dawkins makes the objection with eloquence and a very sharp edge. The belief in God has "great psychological appeal," Dawkins writes, because it "suggests that injustices in this world may be rectified in the next. The 'everlasting arms' hold out a cushion against our own inadequacies which, like a doctor's placebo, is none the less effective for being imaginary." He describes the Christian understanding of hell in precisely the opposite terms, as a threat that men and women "will suffer ghastly torments after death if they do not obey the priestly rules. This is a peculiarly nasty technique of persuasion," Dawkins concludes, "causing great psychological anguish throughout the middle ages and even today. But it is highly effective."[4]

Materialists have several different answers to the question of just where the belief in heaven came from. Some suspect that the belief in heaven, like the ubiquitous belief in God or gods, has genetic origins, whereas others (like Dawkins) posit that it gets passed from one generation to the next through cultural mechanisms.

Both are convinced that Christians who believe in heaven are motivated by the prospect of a heavenly reward. Materialists themselves put no stock in the seventeenth-century French philosopher and mathematician Blaise Pascal's contention—known as Pascal's wager—that any reasonable person should accept Christianity if there is any possibility that its promise of heaven is true, since the downside of being wrong is small and the benefits of being right infinite. But they suspect that millions of others think in Pascal-like terms, clinging to the promise of an eternal reward.

I think they're wrong about this. Even if Christians were convinced that there is no heaven, most would still believe in the truth of Christianity. Christianity's explanations of our idea-making capacity and each of the other puzzles of our existence would still be compelling and would help us to make sense of the complexity of our existence. Bill Stuntz wrote during his treatment for cancer that "even if there were no heaven, no afterlife of any kind, I would feel driven to make of my diseases something good, even at the cost of yielding my own life sooner. I believe that's God's image in me, which I lack the power to eradicate."[5]

Indeed, Pascal's own musings can be read as concerned with the implications of our beliefs about the universe for our lives now, rather than solely with the prospect of an eternal reward. Our lives and relationships will be far richer, Pascal believed, if we consider the possibility (or better still, believe) that a personal God created the universe, rather than living as if the universe is simply atoms and the void.

But let us suppose for a moment that the promise of heavenly rewards is the key reason that Christians believe in Christianity. Even if this were so, it would not demonstrate that Christianity is untrue. Consider, by way of comparison, how we might respond if an Apple executive assured us that Apple's iPhone is vastly superior to other smartphones. We would not simply take her word for it, and we might even be a little skeptical. After all, the executive's paycheck and her future will be bigger and brighter if the iPhone succeeds. But she may be right about the iPhone's superiority. If considerable evidence supports the executive's conclusion, it would be silly to reject the conclusion simply because of her self-interest.

There is a second problem with the suggestion that Christianity should be dismissed because its adherents are attracted by the promise of eternal life. This line of reasoning assumes that the desire for a reward is always a dubious motive for doing or believing something. But it isn't—at least not always. It all depends on the reward in question. To borrow a metaphor from C. S. Lewis, we call a person a gold digger if she attaches herself to someone who is rich or likely to become rich, hoping to marry him and to share in the riches. But we do not look askance if a person expends equal energy and ingenuity in a quest to persuade someone with whom she is deeply in love to marry her. The reward of marriage is an appropriate reward for those who are in love. The same reasoning applies with heaven. It may be crass to long for heaven if a person is looking for a reason to turn her back on the world, but it is altogether different if she longs to be reconciled to and in relationship with God, not just in this life but for eternity.[6]

To be sure, few Christians can honestly say that escape never crosses their minds when they think of heaven. But even here, as Lewis also pointed out, we should not immediately assume that the desire for heaven is suspect. Let me give two examples, one old and one new. The first comes from a case that many law students learn in their first year of law school. A boy's uncle promised to give him a large sum of money on his twenty-first birthday if the boy refrained from swearing or drinking until that time. In the beginning, the boy forswore alcohol and salty language because he wanted the money, but over time his perspective shifted, and he increasingly saw a life of temperance as its own reward. The hope that this would be so was why the uncle originally made the promise.

The second illustration, considerably more common today, is the service projects that many American students undertake prior to college. One high school girl I know spent her summer assisting doctors and nurses in a rickety hospital in Malawi. Other students go to Haiti or other areas where many are suffering. The reward that inspires many of these students has very little to do with serving. They're aiming for college, and they know that an impressive experience can bolster their college applications. But some students develop a genuine passion for global health or disaster relief. Their mercenary desires give way in time to more admirable ones.

This is how the promise of heaven works for Christians. Perhaps there are some who make a Pascal's wager calculation, committing themselves to Christianity because Jesus promises eternal life to those who follow him. But the commitment is likely to be fleeting, and indeed may not be a commitment at all, if it is based wholly on a rational calculation. Much more common is a mixture of motives, including a longing for escape, fears about the consequences of estrangement from God, if there is indeed a God, and the desire to live as Jesus called his followers to live. Over time, Christians often find that the mixture of desires shifts, much as with the student who develops a passion for global health. The afterlife comes to seem less an escape from our earthly lives and more like a purer and more beautiful discipleship. It is an altogether different reward.

Where's the Evidence of Heaven?

Even if materialists or other non-Christians are persuaded that Christianity does not teach that heaven is a place just above the earth and that Christians' longing for heaven is not simply wish fulfillment, a very serious objection remains: the unknowability of heaven. Even more than our perceptions of beauty and suffering, heaven does not seem to be empirically verifiable or testable. What is the evidence of heaven?

One tempting source of evidence is reports of near-death experiences. Many people who have had these experiences report seeing visions of a paradise along with a strong sense of peace, suggesting that they will inhabit the paradise after they die. An Oklahoma woman reports having talked with God for nine minutes. "I didn't see hands and feet and a face," she said. "I just saw the most beautiful light."[7] A man I worked with in a restaurant many years ago told me that Jesus appeared to him while he lay in a hospital near death. He admitted that the vision might sound tacky—"Jesus was wearing a white robe and told me I needed to change my life"—but the man was convinced it really was Jesus he had seen. It is possible that some of these experiences are genuine glimpses of heaven, but they do not strike me as particularly strong evidence. The visions often come to those who are severely oxygen deprived. The oxygen deprivation or other consequences of not breathing may well have psychological effects.

Two kinds of evidence from our ordinary lives seem much more compelling. The first is the evidence of our longings. As C. S. Lewis pointed out long ago, the desires we experience as human beings always seem to have a real object. Our hunger, for instance, is not arbitrary. It is a desire that can be satisfied if we have access to food. So too with the desire most of us feel at one time or another for sex. This desire can be satisfied by sex. Just as there is food for hunger and sex for sexual desire, perhaps there is a world in which our desire for heaven also is satisfied.

All of the longings we have considered in this book may thus be a foreshadowing of heaven. Lewis himself experienced these longings with unusual intensity—he referred to the sensation as joy. "If none of my earthly pleasures satisfy it," Lewis wrote, "that does not prove that the universe is a fraud. Probably earthly pleasures were never meant to satisfy it, but only to arouse it, to suggest the real thing."[8]

The other hint of heaven comes from the testimonies of those who have embraced Christianity. Heaven, and the promise of permanent reconciliation with God, is central to the Christian story about who we are and why we were made. It is the culmination of a narrative that begins with creation, includes our rebellion from God, and concludes with permanent reconciliation with God as a result of Jesus' death and resurrection. The testimony of Christians about how embracing Christianity has changed their lives is thus evidence of the reality of heaven. Even if heaven were simply an escape from the lives we live now, the testimonies of those who embrace Christianity and whose lives are transformed would tell us something about the reality of heaven. The evidence is even more compelling if heaven—and the afterlife—is a dimension of our lives that we can experience in part even now. I believe that it is and that the continuity between life and the afterlife can help explain one of heaven's most puzzling features.

Why Is Heaven So Dull?

Nearly everyone who encounters a Renaissance painting of heaven and hell in an art history course or on a tour of the cathedrals and museums of Europe notices an odd feature of these paintings: hell is almost always far more interesting than heaven. Its agonies seem real and the people familiar; heaven, by contrast, is filled with white-robed figures who have a great deal of time on their hands. Why is heaven so dull?

One possible answer is that we simply cannot imagine what heaven is like. The Bible does not tell us a great deal about heaven, and the few glimpses we get have a metaphorical quality that suggests heaven is beyond our comprehension. The streets of heaven are described as paved with pure gold and its walls as bedecked in jewels. The over-the-top images hint that heaven will have qualities we simply cannot fathom.

No doubt this is part of the explanation, but I do not think it can be the whole story. After all, each of the things I have just said about heaven is also true of hell: the Bible gives us only glimpses, and the picture presented is highly metaphorical, with a lake of sulfurous fire and the gnashing of teeth. Yet artists seem to have far less trouble picking up where the Bible leaves off when they are imagining hell.

I suspect this is because they—and we—have seen the ingenuity with which men and women inflict pain on one another, and we realize that we have this capacity ourselves. Some artists may depict cruelty and atrocities they would be tempted to commit, or have imagined committing but have resisted. It is far harder to imagine what it would be like to lack these impulses. The intricacies of evil are more familiar, and for this reason easier for us to imagine both in ordinary and in magnified form.

At this point an additional assumption often seems to creep in. We assume that because hell is intricate, at least as we imagine it, heaven won't be. Because complexity and devious behavior seem to go hand in hand, heaven will be characterized by purity and simplicity. The rough places will be made smooth, the reasoning goes, the tangles removed. It is therefore no surprise that the heavenly figures in Renaissance paintings often look a trifle bland.

The funny thing about these assumptions is that there is almost no basis for them. Nowhere does the Bible suggest that heaven will require us to leave complexity behind. The more we know about the universe, which the Bible describes as good, the more complex we know it to be. Complexity abounds both at a microscopic and a macroscopic level, from the elegance of the double helix that serves as the building block of life and the mysteries of quantum physics to the intricacies of cosmic phenomena. There is no reason to believe that this complexity will simply disappear in the afterlife.

There is even less reason to believe that human complexity will disappear. I cannot resist giving an illustration from my own line of work here. Nearly everyone assumes that if treachery and deceit disappeared, lawyers would no longer be necessary. Lawyers' principal role seems to be to represent clients who have been harmed, are embroiled in a conflict of one kind or another, or are accused of having violated the law themselves. Lawyers often seem to contribute to the conflicts, which is one reason for the proliferation of jokes suggesting, among other things, that the only difference between lawyers and laboratory rats is that no one becomes attached to lawyers. Grant Gilmore, a famous twentieth-century law professor, once speculated, only half in jest, that "in Heaven there will be no law" but "in Hell there will be nothing but law, and due process will be meticulously observed."[9]

Yet dealing with conflict is only part of what lawyers do. A large portion of many lawyers' practice consists of activities that can be described as navigating complexity. When a lawyer structures a sophisticated transaction or helps a young entrepreneur obtain the licenses he needs to start a new business, she helps him address complexities that might otherwise prove daunting. The prospect of conflict or misbehavior sometimes contributes to the complexity, but the complexity would not disappear even if conflict and misbehavior were absent. If heaven has anything in common with the world as we know it, I think lawyers will be needed to help navigate complexity. The same will be true of architects, artists and even politicians. Like the universe itself, human interaction surely will continue to include the marvelous, the serendipitous and the uncertain.

I should acknowledge that the speculations of several fine contemporary philosophers about what immortality would be like might seem to call these conclusions into question. In an essay called "The Makropulos Case: Reflections on the Tedium of Immortality," Bernard Williams concluded that our lives would eventually flatline into a world of endless boredom if human beings lived forever.[10] More recently, Samuel Scheffler reached a similar conclusion based on somewhat different reasoning. The richness we associate with ordinary life would not be possible, Scheffler argues, for creatures

> who pass through no stages of life, who know nothing of the characteristic challenges, triumphs, or disasters associated with any of those stages, who need not work to survive, who do not undergo danger or overcome it, who do not age or face death or the risk of it, who do not experience the reactions of grief and loss that the death of a loved one inspires, and who never have to make what they can of the limited time and opportunities that they have been given.[11]

Complexity is not possible, in Scheffler's view, in a world that no longer has scarcity and tragic choices.

As wise and sensible as these philosophers are, they seem to me to underestimate the scope of our idea-making capacity. Even if we do not experience adolescence, emerging adulthood and old age in heaven, there is no reason to believe that all nuance will disappear. We are endlessly inventive and complex creatures. Despite the absence of scarcity and stages of life, our lives could be "composed of an endless sequence of quests, undertakings, and discoveries, including successes and failures," as Thomas Nagel puts it.[12] During the course of human history, our circumstances have changed radically, but we have always adjusted and mapped out new challenges, as Nagel also notes. This surely would continue to be true in a world that has been transformed, especially if we truly are made in the image of God, as Christians believe.

If I am right about this, it suggests a different reason why heaven is so difficult to portray in art: heaven may in some respects be more of the same, more of what comes naturally for idea-making men and women, rather than a complete departure from life as we know it now.

For precisely this reason, my own favorite painting of the afterlife is the Stefaneschi Triptych, an unassuming altarpiece painted in the late thirteenth century by Giotto, one of the pioneers of Renaissance art. This painting can be found in the Vatican Picture Gallery, a much less heavily trafficked part of the Vatican than the Sistine Chapel. The painting consists of three wood panels, each of which is wide at the bottom and narrows to a point at the top. The large center panel shows a resplendent, cobalt-blue-robed Christ in all his redemptive, post-resurrection power, while the small side panels depict the gruesome deaths of Peter and Paul. On the left, Peter is crucified upside down, and on the right Paul's head lies a few feet away from his decapitated body, while colorful crowds of onlookers survey the scenes. In each of the panels, angels flutter like birds above the dying saints, with the squinting eyes and sculpted expressions that are characteristic of Giotto's angels.

The first time I encountered the painting, my eyes drifted back and forth from the tormented bodies to the angels treading the air in melancholy silence. Only then did I notice the rest of the story, the small figures at the top of each panel: Peter appears on the left and Paul on the right. They have the same faces as below, the same clothing even, but they have been made whole—in Paul's case quite literally; his head is reattached to his body. And they are resplendent like Christ.

What makes Giotto's portrayal seem so real, at least for me, is seeing both points in time in the same painting, not just one. The same body that is wracked by the torments that come in the world in which we live is made new by the one who came to make all things new. That's how heaven will be, I think, for anyone who trusts in Christ's promises. Heaven isn't some distant location where disembodied souls gather. It's our bodies and our world transformed. It all belongs in the same picture.

The most beautiful musical depictions of heaven have many of the same qualities. Some of the loveliest examples are spirituals composed by American slaves prior to the Civil War. In "Swing Low, Sweet Chariot," a lead singer sings the first line and the congregation answers with a repeated refrain:

Swing low, sweet chariot
   Coming for to carry me home
Swing low, sweet chariot
   Coming for to carry me home
If you get there before I do
   Coming for to carry me home
Tell all my friends, I'm coming too
   Coming for to carry me home

In one sense, these verses speak of the singers' desire for union with God after they die, in terms that a slave master who heard the singing would be hard pressed to condemn. But in another sense, the singers long for an escape to an earthly freedom in the here and now (and in fact, the singing of these verses was sometimes used as the signal that the hour had come to flee on the Underground Railroad). Christians believe that heaven will bring both of these things: union with God and a transformation of the world we know now.

Glimpses of Beauty and Justice

Although I have emphasized the human dimension of heaven, Christianity teaches that the transformation that is to come will include the entire creation, not just us. Paul writes in his letter to the Romans, for instance, that "the creation itself will be liberated from its bondage to decay" (Romans 8:21 NIV). If the creation will one day be restored to its intended condition, the glimpses and hints of beauty and justice that we experience may have permanent significance.

Consider a few of the towering achievements of the Western tradition—such as Bach's Brandenburg concertos—that are universally recognized as works of genius and beauty. If beauty is indeed a central feature of the universe as it is intended to be, Bach's music may well delight and inspire forever. So too with Michelangelo's Sistine Chapel and perhaps some of Balanchine's most beautiful ballets. If we turn from beauty to justice, William Wilberforce's decades-long campaign to overturn slavery in England and Martin Luther King's civil rights movement in America are achievements on a similar scale.

Of course, Bach and King cannot be found in the Bible, but, interestingly enough, the passages that speak of heaven include references that seem to have just the same quality. As the theologian Richard Mouw has pointed out, according to the prophet Isaiah, whose prophesies are echoed in the New Testament accounts of heaven, "the ships of Tarshish" and the "glory of Lebanon" will each have a place in the heavenly city. These references were as instantly recognizable to those who lived in the ancient Near East as Bach and Michelangelo are to us now. The ships of Tarshish were marvels of ancient technology, seagoing vessels that crisscrossed the known world, and the glory of Lebanon was its cedars and the craftsmen who fashioned them into some of the most beautiful objects and buildings of the ancient world.[13]

At the end of an essay called "The Weight of Glory," C. S. Lewis pointed out that, if Christianity is true, "there are no *ordinary* people." We are destined for eternity. "It is a serious thing," Lewis wrote, "to live in a society of gods and goddesses, to remember that the dullest and most uninteresting person you can talk to may one day be a creature which, if you saw it now, you would be strongly tempted to worship, or else a horror and a corruption such as you now meet, if at all, only in a nightmare."[14] As beautiful and as true as these sentences are, I think Lewis could have gone even farther. The new heavens and new earth will indeed be peopled by those who have been reconciled with God, but the new creation will be more than just people. It will blossom with the beautiful objects and words they created and with the justice they achieved.

Imperfection Perfected

I do not mean to suggest, of course, that visionaries like Bach or Michelangelo or King were perfect. Thanks to the endless flow of revisionist biographies, the flaws of their lives are well known. Even their works of genius may need to be perfected still further and the imperfections removed. In one of the New Testament Epistles, Paul suggests that his own works and the works of other leaders in the early church will be tested by fire. Their flawed or inconsequential features will be burned like stubble, so that only the precious metals—their most valuable dimensions—remain (1 Corinthians 3:13-15). All of the beauty and justice we have been considering will undergo the same kind of testing, so that only the precious portions endure.

It is tempting to conclude that the testing has already begun and that our earthly existence is marching slowly—or perhaps even rapidly—toward perfection. But the testing, and the lines of continuity between this life and the next, do not tell us anything one way or another about the general trajectory of beauty and justice. Some of the most splendid works of art have been created in bleak times, and justice often is most visible against a backdrop of injustice.

As our recent history attests, this should come as a comfort. We certainly can point to progress in some areas. Steven Pinker has documented a striking decline in human violence over the last several centuries. In the United States, racial justice has vastly improved since the height of the civil rights movement, when King spoke in his "I Have a Dream" speech of having to tell his daughter that "Funtown," an amusement park she'd seen on TV, was not open for her. But in other areas, such as poverty in our cities and towns, the progress is harder to see; and still others—the stability of marriages and families is an obvious example—have seen marked deterioration. But in all of these areas, whether the overall picture is characterized by progress or regress, there have been contributions of eternal significance.

What Difference Does Heaven Make?

I should acknowledge that not all Christians would agree with the picture of heaven I have been developing. Some do assume that the earth will simply be destroyed, as reflected in the popular series of Left Behind novels and the familiar bumper sticker saying, "In case of rapture, this car will be unmanned." But most Christians have always believed not only that our physical bodies will be resurrected, but also that the earth and the cosmos will be transformed. Jesus began the process with his own life and resurrection, and he will one day complete it.

The contemporary theologian who has done more than any other to explain this feature of Christian thought is N. T. Wright. Drawing in part on the picture of heaven at the end of the Bible (Revelation 21–22), Wright argues that heaven and earth are neither "poles apart, needing to be separated forever," nor are they "simply different ways of looking at the same thing, as would be implied by some kinds of pantheism." He concludes, "No, they are radically different, but they are made for each other in the same way (Revelation is suggesting) as male and female."

If the current world will be transformed, rather than destroyed, the contributions we make to beauty and justice, no matter how small, have eternal significance. Wright states,

> What you *do* in the present by painting, preaching, singing, sewing, praying, teaching, building hospitals, digging wells,

campaigning for justice, writing poems, caring for the needy, loving your neighbor as yourself—*will last into God's future.* These activities are not simply ways of making the present life a little less beastly, a little more bearable. . . . They are part of what we may call *building for God's kingdom.*[15]

Notice how this Christian perspective differs from that of a materialist. For a materialist, the universe is impermanent. Current scientific evidence suggests that the universe will eventually collapse, and it is possible that our world will be destroyed much sooner by a nuclear or environmental catastrophe or by a freak disaster like the asteroid that is thought to have ended the era of the dinosaurs. When a materialist thinks deeply about these issues, he cannot help concluding that any contributions he or others make to beauty or justice are fragile and will ultimately disappear.

I do not mean to suggest that materialists have no reason to care about the future. Most do not assume that the world will end tomorrow, and they feel a stake in the future because they have children or for other reasons. But for a materialist, the world is a clock that will one day stop ticking.

Christianity teaches that an eternal future stretches before us. This means that at least some of the contributions we and those around us make to beauty and justice will last forever. I often imagine what some of these contributions may be. Many of my law students are familiar with an organization called the International Justice Mission. Founded by a lawyer named Gary Haugen in 1997, it comes to the aid of victims of sexual trafficking and other forms of slavery, often by prodding local authorities to enforce laws that are already on the books. Others contribute to beauty and justice in more ordinary ways. Here in Philadelphia, where I live, a small group of lawyers provides free services for clients who've gotten entangled in legal issues of one kind or another and cannot afford to hire a lawyer. A couple who run an architecture firm from their house have added touches of beauty to our house and many other houses and buildings in our region. Christianity teaches that even the smallest of these efforts may have eternal value.

Several years ago, I had breakfast with a Christian scholar I'll call Deb in the university town where she lives. Deb was a nurse before she first went to graduate school, then changed careers and wound up as a tenured professor at a top university. But Deb's life was jolted beyond recognition when her closest friend died suddenly and horribly from meningitis. After the loss of this friend—whom Deb describes as having been her "soul mate"—Deb struggled to regain her professional stride; a funk settled over her life that wouldn't seem to lift.

Deb told me that reflecting on heaven and the afterlife—spurred by Wright's book *Surprised by Hope*—helped her recover from the shock of losing her dearest friend and rejuvenated her personal and professional life. It helped her, she said, to understand more fully why the work she does—her teaching, her writing, her relationships with students—matters. "While it is a mystery exactly how," she wrote a few months after our breakfast in a testimonial describing her new thinking, "the new heavens and the new earth will have some continuity with the earth we now inhabit":

> The knowledge that the new heavens and the new earth will be physical and it will have some continuity with the earthly creation I have come to know and love puts a whole new spin on

everything I do. I am part of an eternal renovation project that Jesus inaugurated by His early ministry and resurrection. If I am seeking to further the values of the Kingdom of God then I can be in the stream of restoration that he is already doing.

Some readers may remember a song by Belinda Carlisle proclaiming that "heaven is a place on earth."[16] Christians believe that heaven is more than simply a place on Earth. But Christians also believe that here on Earth is where heaven and the afterlife begin.

EPILOGUE

When I give talks on the subjects we have just explored, one or two people usually come up afterward and ask how to consider Christianity further. My answer always has four parts. Although it is framed with those who are new to Christianity in mind, in my view it is equally relevant for those of us who have been Christians for many years and for those who are not Christians but are quite familiar with Christianity.

First, keep reading. There are excellent articles and books on most of the issues that I have discussed in this book, many of which go into much more detail than I have had space for here. The sources cited here will give you some idea of the books that I find particularly useful, both on Christianity in general and on specific issues. No one can read everything about everything, of course, so it often makes sense to focus on the issues you find most interesting or troubling. With some of the deepest issues—such as the problem of evil or the relationship between Christianity and evolutionary theory—it can be counterproductive to dabble. The best approach may be to read widely if the issue concerns you and not to worry about it if it doesn't. That was the advice I was given many years ago, and I have found it to be very good advice.

Second, if you haven't done so, spend some time in church. When I first started thinking about Christianity in college, I was fairly shy, but when acquaintances or friends mentioned that they went to church, I often asked if I could come along with them some Sunday. No one ever said no, and I found it a great way to see what all the fuss was about. Christianity is relational and communal, not just intellectual. Christians believe, for instance, that in some mysterious way, those who have embraced the reconciliation with God that Jesus offers are the "body of Christ." If Christianity is true, that truth will be reflected (dimly at times, but discernibly) in the testimonies of individual Christians and in the Christian community. The best way to see this is to step inside a church. For those who have grown frustrated with the institutional church, this may mean giving it another try.

Third, find a Christian whom you respect and who is willing to answer the questions you have about Christianity and what Christians do and do not believe. This is the one piece of advice that I did not follow myself until much later, and have often regretted. The best sounding board is often someone who is older and can share his or her thinking and experience, but it can also be someone closer to your age or even much younger who has the same qualities. I recently heard a thirtysomething New Yorker tell of his relationship with a ninety-year-old former professor of his who developed a passion for Christianity late in life. He is her mentor with Christianity, and she his in many other areas.

Finally, read the Bible itself. There is no substitute for reading the text that Christians believe to be true. Many readers find it most helpful to read the New Testament first, then go back and read the Old Testament. I personally took the opposite tack, starting at page 1 of the Old Testament. Either way, if you've never read the entire Bible, I would encourage you to commit to reading a few pages each day until you have.

One of the best things about these four little bits of advice is that they are a no-lose proposition. Even if you eventually find yourself unconvinced, you are sure to meet some interesting people, to better understand the faith that has shaped so much literature and social life, and to think through issues that each of us should think through at some point in his or her life. If you find yourself persuaded, or re-persuaded, that Christianity is true, and if your experience is anything like mine, you will find that you are in for the adventure of a lifetime—and beyond.

ACKNOWLEDGMENTS

B ill Stuntz and I originally hoped to write this book (or one like it) together. Bill sent me an initial set of notes in October 2008, and we went back and forth for a month or so after that. If Bill's cancer treatments were successful, we planned to start as soon as he finished *The Collapse of American Criminal Justice*, the monumental book he was working on. But the cancer got worse. Shortly before he died, Bill told me our book was the one project he was most sorry he wouldn't be able to finish. I still talk to Bill in my mind, and I am grateful that I can talk in person to his remarkable wife, Ruth Stuntz (as well as Sarah, Sam and Andy), and for her help on this project.

After Bill's death in March 2011, the project stayed on hold until the following year, when I was invited to moderate a Veritas Forum event titled "Is Anything Worth Believing In?" with Oxford math professor John Lennox at the University of Pennsylvania. After the event Patrick Arsenault, a materialist postdoctoral student at Penn's medical school, sent me an email thanking me for my role.

This led to coffee and a friendly debate about the plausibility of Christianity. After several more of these conversations, I decided that perhaps it was time to dust off my notes and just start writing the book. Patrick gave me extensive, often skeptical, comments on the entire manuscript, and has been the ideal interlocutor throughout.

Veritas Forum also was involved from the beginning, especially Bethany Yu, director of publishing and communications. Bethany read the earliest and subsequent drafts of every chapter, edited, offered encouragement, suggested ideas and more. Many paragraphs of the book are ideas, and often words, that came directly from Bethany. When the time came to submit the proposal to InterVarsity Press, David Hobbet, the chief executive of Veritas, offered a full-throated and essential endorsement. Rebecca McLaughlin has worked closely with me on talks related to the book, as have others at Veritas Forum. Thanks too to Curtis Chang, Dan Cho, Andy Crouch and Michael Lindsay for the crucial affirmation of Veritas Riff.

Al Hsu, my editor at InterVarsity Press, has been a steady hand throughout, starting with a thirteen-page, single-spaced memo sharpening and critiquing nearly every page of the manuscript. Despite a very fast publication process, many friends and colleagues read and commented on the manuscript, including Stephen Adams, Lincoln Caplan, Emanuele Conte, John DiIulio, Bill Draper, Karl Johnson, Tim Keller, Elizabeth Knoll, Jonathan Master, Stephen Master, Robert Miller, Mark Noll, Marvin Olasky, Krystal Smith, Richard Squire, Paul Watkins, John Wilson and Jonathan Yu. I found their tendency to disagree about which chapters were the best and which needed the most work encouraging, sometimes wearying, and extremely helpful. Grace Lee Baughan, Peter Baughan, Andy Crouch, Dave DeHuff, Jeff Dill, John Grogan, Bob Fryling, Howard Lesnick, Tremper Longman, George McFarland, Peter Moore, Naomi Riley, Phil Ryken, Larry Shapiro and Jim Whitman provided valuable suggestions or conversations at various points in the project, as did participants at the Veritas Forums and other events where many of these ideas were first vetted. Thomas Mack and Ben Thomas provided superb research assistance, and Silvana Burgese and Bill Draper helped in numerous ways. Dean Mike Fitts, who has just left to take the helm of Tulane University, and my colleagues at the University of Pennsylvania Law School have been highly supportive at every juncture.

My wife, Sharon Skeel, a very fine dance historian, vowed to steer clear of this project, but she and our sons, Carter and Stephen, were sounding boards for some of the ideas, sometimes knowingly and sometimes not.

Each of you is in these pages, and for that I am deeply grateful.

NOTES

Preface

[1]Christian Wiman, *My Bright Abyss: Meditation of a Modern Believer* (New York: Farrar, Straus and Giroux, 2013), pp. 154-55.

[2]Ibid., p. 165.

Introduction

[1]Barry Schwartz, *The Paradox of Choice: Why More Is Less* (New York: Harper Perennial, 2004), p. 19; citing S. Iyengar and M. Lepper, "When Choice Is Demotivating: Can One Desire Too Much of a Good Thing?" *Journal of Personality and Social Psychology* 79 (2000): 995-1006.

[2]The debate featured William Lane Craig, a Christian philosopher and apologist at Biola University, and Lawrence Krauss, a physicist at the University of Arizona. A transcript of it can be found at www.reasonablefaith .org/the-craig-krauss-debate-at-north-carolina-state-university.

[3]Nathan Schneider, "The New Theist: How William Lane Craig Became Christian Philosophy's Boldest Apostle," *The Chronicle Review*, July 1, 2013.

[4]William Lane Craig, "God Is Not Dead Yet: How Current Philosophers Argue for His Existence," *Christianity Today*, July 2008 (cover story), www .christianitytoday.com/ct/2008/july/13.22.html?paging=off.

[5]Alvin Plantinga's books on warranted belief have been particularly important in this regard. Alvin Plantinga, *Warranted Christian Belief* (New York: Oxford University Press, 2000).

[6]Val Van Brocklin, "A Trial Is NOT About the Truth," Officer.com, January 18, 2010, www.officer.com/article/10232949/a-trial-is-not-about-the-truth (prosecutor's column).

[7]Alan Dershowitz, "Is the Criminal Trial a Search for Truth?" *Frontline*, October 4, 2005, www.pbs.org/wgbh/pages/frontline/oj/highlights/dershowitz.html.

[8]Phillip E. Johnson, *Darwin on Trial* (Downers Grove, IL: InterVarsity Press, 1991), p. 8, emphasis added.

[9]Josh McDowell, *Evidence That Demands a Verdict* (1972; repr., San Bernardino, CA: Here's Life, 1986); Lee Strobel, *The Case for Christ: A Journalist's Personal Investigation of the Evidence for Jesus* (Grand Rapids: Zondervan, 1998).

[10]*Connecticut Trial Practice*, 2nd ed., vol. 6, Connecticut Practice Series (Thompson Reuters), sect. 6.26.

[11]Jack B. Swerling, "'I Can't Believe I Asked That Question': A Look at Cross-Examination Techniques," *South Carolina Law Review* 50 (1999): 753, 778.

[12]Philip Kitcher, "The Trouble with Scientism," *The New Republic*, May 4, 2012.

[13]Steven Pinker, *The Better Angels of Our Nature: Why Violence Has Declined* (New York: Penguin, 2011), p. 669.

[14]Peter Singer, *The Life You Can Save* (New York: Random House, 2009).

[15]Richard Dawkins, *The God Delusion* (London: Bantam Press, 2006), p. 298.

[16]For a transcript of the debate, see "The Famous 1948 BBC Radio Debate on the Existence of God," Reason Broadcast, http://reasonbroadcast.blogspot.ca/2012/03/debate-on-existence-of-god-by-bertrand.html.

[17]Richard Dawkins, afterword, to Lawrence M. Krauss, *A Universe from Nothing: Why There Is Something Rather than Nothing* (New York: Free Press, 2012), pp. 187, 191.

Chapter 1: Ideas and Idea Making

[1]The one hundred billion estimate can be found in Eric R. Kandel, *The Search for Memory: The Emergence of a New Science of Mind* (New York: Norton, 2007), p. 59.

[2]Thomas Nagel, *Mind and Cosmos: Why the Materialist Neo-Darwinian Conception of Nature Is Almost Certainly False* (New York: Oxford University Press, 2012), p. 53.

[3]Steven Pinker, *How the Mind Works* (New York: Norton, 1997), p. 521.

[4]Ibid., p. 525.

[5]Scott Atran, *In Gods We Trust: The Evolutionary Landscape of Supernatural Agency* (New York: Oxford University Press, 2002).

[6]Jonathan Haidt, *The Righteous Mind: Why Good People Are Divided by Politics and Religion* (New York: Vintage Books, 2013), p. 293.

[7]Scott Atran and Joseph Henrich, "The Evolution of Religion: How Cognitive By-products, Adaptive Learning Heuristics, Ritual Displays, and Group Competition Generate Deep Commitments to Prosocial Religions," *Biological Theory*, 5 (2010): 18-30.

[8]Eugene P. Wigner, "The Unreasonable Effectiveness of Mathematics in the

Natural Sciences," *Communications on Pure and Applied Mathematics* 13 (1960): 1-14. The quote is from p. 3.

[9]Nagel, *Mind and Cosmos*, p. 83.

[10]Acts 22:6-11 (speech to crowd); Acts 26:12-18 (tells Felix and Agrippa the same conversion story); Acts 26:22 (he's had God's help).

[11]St. Augustine of Hippo, *The Confessions of Saint Augustine*, trans. John H. Ryan (New York: Doubleday, 1960), p. 1.

[12]Richard Dawkins, *The Magic of Reality: How We Know What's Really True* (New York: Free Press, 2012).

[13]Olivia Judson, "Why I'm Happy I Evolved," *New York Times*, January 1, 2006, Week in Review, p. 8.

[14]Mandalet de Barco, "Sunday Assembly: A Church for the Godless Picks up Steam," *NPR Morning Edition*, January 7, 2014. Available at www.npr.org.

[15]Quoted in Rodney Stark, *The Rise of Christianity: How the Obscure Marginal Jesus Movement Became the Dominant Religious Force in the Western World in a Few Centuries* (San Francisco: HarperSanFrancisco, 1997), p. 118.

[16]Quoted in John Lennox, *Gunning for God: Why the New Atheists Are Missing the Target* (London: Lion UK, 2011), p. 121 (quoting Dawkins's "New Ten Commandments").

[17]Stark, *The Rise of Christianity*, p. 95.

[18]For evidence on the relationship between the number of premarital partners and divorce, see, for example, Jay Teachman, "Premarital Sex, Premarital Cohabitation, and the Risk of Subsequent Marital Dissolution Among Women," *Journal of Marriage and Family* 65 (2003): 444-55; for evidence on infidelity within the marriage, see, for example, Judith Treas and Deirdre Giesen, "Sexual infidelity among married and cohabiting Americans," *Journal of Marriage and Family* 62, no. 1 (2000): 48-60.

[19]The empirical evidence on marriage is surveyed in extensive detail (including discussion of each of the issues I mention in the text), in Institute for American Values, *Why Marriage Matters*, 2nd ed. (New York: Institute for American Values, 2005).

[20]Ibid., p. 23. Gunilla Ringback Weitoft, Anders Hjern, Bengt Haglund and Mans Rosen, "Mortality, Severe Morbidity, and Injury in Children Living with Single Parents in Sweden: A Population-Based Study," *The Lancet* 361 (2003): 289-95.

[21]Lizette Alvarez, "Strip Clubs in Tampa Are Ready to Cash in on G.O.P. Convention," *New York Times*, July 27, 2002, A11.

[22]Mark A. Noll, *America's God: From Jonathan Edwards to Abraham Lincoln* (New York: Oxford University Press, 2002), p. 392.

[23]Ibid., pp. 386-401. The significance of singling out a particular race is discussed on pp. 419-20.

[24]Mark Noll tells this story, which quotes from Howard Thurman, *Jesus and the Disinherited* (New York: Abingdon-Cokesbury, 1949), in "Have Christians Done More Harm Than Good?" in *Must Christianity Be Violent? Reflections on History, Practice, and Theology*, ed. Kenneth R. Chase and Alan Jacobs (Grand Rapids: Brazos Press, 2003), pp. 79, 86.

[25]Philip Jenkins, *The Next Christendom: The Coming of Global Christianity*, 3rd ed. (New York: Oxford University Press, 2011), p. 72.

[26]Ibid., p. 89.

[27]Nagel, *Mind and Cosmos*, p. 83.

[28]Rebecca F. Elliott, "Faith Emerging: Students Find Christianity at Harvard," *Harvard Crimson*, March 21, 2012.

[29]Jordan Monge, "The Atheist's Dilemma," *Christianity Today*, March 2013, p. 88.

[30]Ibid.

Chapter 2: Beauty and the Arts

[1]Darwin introduced sexual selection in *The Descent of Man, and Selection in Relation to Sex*, 2nd ed. (New York: Hurst & Company, 1874).

[2]Quoted in Adam Kirsch, "Art Over Biology," *The New Republic*, August 2, 2012, pp. 39, 40.

[3]Stephen Jay Gould and Richard C. Lewontin, "The Spandrels of San Marco and the Panglossian Paradigm: A Critique of the Adaptionist Programme," *Proceedings of the Royal Society of London*, series B, 205 (1979): 581-98.

[4]Steven Pinker, *How the Mind Works* (New York: Norton, 1997), p. 524.

[5]Ibid., p. 537.

[6]Ibid., p. 376.

[7]Mark Pagel, *Wired for Culture: Origins of the Human Social Mind* (New York: Norton, 2013), quoted in Kirsh, "Art Over Biology," p. 42.

[8]William Wordsworth, "Lines Composed a Few Miles Above Tintern Abbey," in *The Selected Poetry and Prose of Wordsworth*, ed. Geoffrey F. Hartman (New York: Meridian, 1980), pp. 101, 104 (lines 93-99).

[9]Michaeleen Doucleff, "Anatomy of a Tear-Jerker," *Wall Street Journal*, February 11, 2012.

[10]See, for example, Stephen J. Morse, "Avoiding Irrational NeuroLaw Exuberance: A Plea for Neuromodesty," *Mercer Law Review* 62 (2011): 837. See also p. 851.

[11]Quoted in R. W. Sharples, *Stoics, Epicureans and Sceptics: An Introduction to Hellenistic Philosophy* (London: Routledge, 1996), p. 56.

[12]C. S. Lewis, *Mere Christianity* (Nashville: Broadman & Holman, 1980), p. 51 (first published in 1952).

[13]Harold Bloom, *The American Religion: The Emergence of the Post-Christian Nation* (New York: Touchstone Books, 1992).

[14]T. V. F. Brogan, "The New Criticism," in *The New Princeton Encyclopedia of Poetry and Poetics*, ed. Alex Preminger and T. V. F. Brogan (Princeton: Princeton University Press, 1993), p. 833.

[15]Nicholas Wolterstorff, *Art in Action: Toward a Christian Aesthetic* (Grand Rapids: Eerdmans, 1980), pp. 164-68.

[16]St. Augustine of Hippo, *The Trinity*, trans. Edmund Hill (Brooklyn: New City Press, 1991).

[17]See, for example, N. T. Wright, *After You Believe: Why Christian Character Matters* (New York: HarperCollins, 2010), p. 139.

[18]Andy Crouch, *Culture Making: Recovering Our Creative Calling* (Downers Grove, IL: InterVarsity Press, 2008), pp. 90-96.

[19]Daniel A. Siedell, "The Dark Light of Thomas Kinkade," Patheos, May 22, 2012, www.patheos.com/blogs/cultivare/author/danielsiedell.

[20]H. Buxton Forman, ed., *The Complete Poetical Works of John Keats* (New York: Oxford University Press, 1934), p. 234.

[21]Elaine Scarry, *On Beauty: And Being Just* (Princeton, NJ: Princeton University Press, 1999), p. 31.

[22]Ibid., pp. 30, 31.

[23]Robert Alter, *Genesis* (New York: Norton, 1996), pp. xv, xvi.

[24]Mihaly Csikszentmihalyi, *Flow: The Psychology of Optimal Experience* (New York: Harper and Row, 1990).

[25]Andrew Newberg and Eugene D'Aquili, *Why God Won't Go Away: Brain Science and the Biology of Belief* (New York: Ballantine Books, 2002). Newberg and D'Aquili describe their imaging experiments in the first chapter.

[26]C. S. Lewis, *Till We Have Faces: A Novel of Cupid and Psyche* (New York: Houghton Mifflin Harcourt, 1980), p. 74.

Chapter 3: Suffering and Sensation

[1]Lincoln Caplan, "Appreciation: William Stuntz," *New York Times*, March 24, 2011, A30.

[2]David Hume, *Dialogues Concerning Natural Religion*, ed. Richard Popkin (Indianapolis: Hackett, 1980), p. 63.

[3]John K. Ryan, trans., *The Confessions of Saint Augustine* (New York: Doubleday, 1960), p. 43 (bk. 3, chap. 7).

[4]C. S. Lewis, *The Problem of Pain* (San Francisco: HarperSanFrancisco, 2000), pp. 22-24.

[5]Richard Dawkins, *The Greatest Show on Earth: The Evidence for Evolution* (New York: Free Press, 2009), p. 395.

[6]Marcus Aurelius, *Meditations,* ed. Maxwell Staniforth (1964; repr. New York: Barnes & Noble, 1996), p. 64.

[7]Christopher Hitchens, *Mortality* (New York: Twelve, 2012), p. 1. The second quote is from p. 3.

[8]Ibid., p. 69.

[9]William J. Stuntz, *Painful Living,* unpublished manuscript, p. 2. At a celebration of his career in 2010, Stuntz remarked, after having been described as the scholarly equivalent of a great baseball player, that the only thing he and Barry Bonds had in common was the use of drugs that are illegal without a prescription.

[10]Hitchens, *Mortality,* p. 97.

[11]William J. Stuntz, "Living Weak," Less Than the Least, www.law.upenn .edu/blogs/dskeel/archives/2008/05/living_weakstuntz.html#more.

[12]Hitchens, *Mortality,* p. 37.

[13]Ibid., pp. 6, 13.

[14]Christopher Hitchens, *God Is Not Great: How Religion Poisons Everything* (New York: Twelve, 2007), p. 18.

[15]Hitches, *Mortality,* pp. 11, 4, 8.

[16]Stuntz, *Painful Living,* p. 28.

[17]William J. Stuntz, "Three Gifts for Hard Times," *Christianity Today,* August 2009, pp. 44, 46.

[18]William J. Stuntz, private correspondence, 2008.

[19]Stuntz, "Three Gifts," p. 46 (emphasis in original).

[20]Stuntz, private correspondence, 2008.

[21]Timothy Keller, *Walking with God Through Pain and Suffering* (New York: Dutton, 2013), pp. 205-21. Keller calls this chapter "Varieties of Suffering."

[22]Hitchens, *Mortality,* pp. 40-41.

[23]Stuntz, "Pain and Ugliness," Less Than the Least, March 2, 2008, www.law .upenn.edu/blogs/dskeel/archives/2008/03/pain_and_ugliness_stuntz.html.

[24]*Final Harvest: Emily Dickinson's Poems* (Boston: Little, Brown and Company, 1961), p. 177 (no. 290).

[25]Rachel Marie Stone, "A Good Death," *Books & Culture,* January/February 2014, p. 5.

[26]Timothy Keller, *The Reason for God: Belief in an Age of Skepticism* (New York: Dutton, 2008), p. 30.

[27]Douglas Martin, "W. J. Stuntz, Who Stimulated Legal Minds, Dies at 52," *New York Times,* March 21, 2011, A23, www.nytimes.com/2011/03/21/us/21stuntz .html?_r=0. The picture, by Melissa Gilstrap, is reprinted (without the citation

to Job) on the dedication page. I am especially grateful to Melissa for permission to use the image.

[28]Stuntz, "Three Gifts," p. 47.

Chapter 4: The Justice Paradox

[1]T. S. Eliot, *The Social Function of Poetry* (1945 ed.), quoted in Thomas C. Grey, *The Wallace Stevens Case: Law and the Practice of Poetry* (Cambridge, MA: Harvard University Press, 1991), p. 103, emphasis in original.

[2]William J. Stuntz, *The Collapse of American Criminal Justice* (Cambridge, MA: Harvard University Press, 2011), p. 34.

[3]J. S. Mill, *On Liberty*, ed. Gertrude Himmelfarb (New York: Penguin, 1984), first published in 1859; John Rawls, *A Theory of Justice* (Cambridge, MA: Harvard University Press, 1971).

[4]Richard Dawkins, *The Selfish Gene*, rev. ed. (Oxford: Oxford University Press, 1989), pp. 200-201.

[5]Steven Pinker, "Science Is Not Your Enemy," *The New Republic*, August 6, 2013, p. 4.

[6]Stuntz, *The Collapse*, p. 1.

[7]Steven Pinker, *The Better Angels of Our Nature: Why Violence Has Declined* (New York: Penguin, 2011), p. 692.

[8]For a general summary of the trials and their abuses, see James Montgomery Boice and Philip Graham Ryken, *Jesus on Trial* (Wheaton, IL: Crossway Books, 2002).

[9]David A. Skeel Jr. and William J. Stuntz, "Christianity and the (Modest) Rule of Law," *University of Pennsylvania Journal of Constitutional Law* 8 (2006): 809-40; David A. Skeel Jr., "The Unbearable Lightness of Christian Legal Scholarship," *Emory Law Journal* 57 (2008): 1471-525.

[10]William J. Stuntz, "Law and Grace," *University of Virginia Law Review* 98 (2012): 367. The discussion in this paragraph and the next draws from this article.

[11]Quoted in Christopher H. Evans, *The Kingdom Is Always but Coming: A Life of Walter Rauschenbusch* (Grand Rapids: Eerdmans, 2004), p. 107.

[12]See, for example, Rodney Stark, *The Victory of Reason: How Christianity Led to Freedom, Capitalism, and Western Success* (New York: Random House, 2005).

Chapter 5: Life and Afterlife

[1]John W. Loftus, ed., *The Christian Delusion: Why Faith Fails* (New York: Prometheus Books, 2010), p. 132.

[2]C. S. Lewis, *Reflections on the Psalms* (New York: Harcourt, Brace & Company, 1958), p. 63.

[3]John O'Neil, "Equation of Time Solves Mystery of Gray Mornings," *New York Times*, January 15, 2013.

[4]Richard Dawkins, *The Selfish Gene*, rev. ed. (Oxford: Oxford University Press, 1989), pp. 193, 197.

[5]William Stuntz, email correspondence to David Skeel, November 21, 2008.

[6]C. S. Lewis, "The Weight of Glory," in *The Weight of Glory and Other Addresses* (New York: Macmillan, 1980), p. 4. Lewis uses the example of a schoolboy learning Greek to make the point I make in the next paragraph.

[7]Carol Kuruvilla, "Oklahoma woman shares near-death experience of dying and talking with God for nine minutes," *New York Daily News*, April 3, 2013, www.nydailynews.com/news/national/oklahoma-woman-shares-near-death-experience-meeting-god-article-1.1307226.

[8]C. S. Lewis, *Mere Christianity* (Nashville: Broadman & Holman, 1980), p. 121. First published in 1952.

[9]Grant Gilmore, *The Ages of American Law* (New Haven, CT: Yale University Press, 1978), p. 110.

[10]"The Makropulos Case: Reflections on the Tedium of Immortality," in Bernard Williams, *Problems of the Self* (Cambridge: Cambridge University Press, 1973), pp. 82-100.

[11]Samuel Scheffler, *Death and the Afterlife* (New York: Oxford University Press, 2013), pp. 98-99.

[12]Thomas Nagel, "After You're Gone," *New York Review of Books*, January 9, 2014, pp. 26-27.

[13]Richard J. Mouw, *When the Kings Come Marching In: Isaiah and the New Jerusalem* (Grand Rapids: Eerdmans, 2002).

[14]C. S. Lewis, "The Weight of Glory," in *The Weight of Glory and Other Addresses* (New York: Macmillan, 1980), pp. 3, 18-19, emphasis in original.

[15]N. T. Wright, *Surprised by Hope* (New York: HarperOne, 2008), p. 193, emphasis in original.

[16]For a similar use of Carlisle's song, see Andy Crouch, *Culture Making: Recovering Our Creative Calling* (Downers Grove, IL: InterVarsity Press, 2008), p. 170.

INDEX

VERITAS· Books
FROM INTERVARSITY PRESS

As a partnership between The Veritas Forum and InterVarsity Press, Veritas Books connect the pursuit of knowledge with the deepest questions of life and truth. Established and emerging Christian thinkers grapple with challenging issues, offering academically rigorous and responsible scholarship that contributes to current and ongoing discussions in the university world. Veritas Books are written in the spirit of genuine dialogue, addressing particular academic disciplines as well as topics of broad interest for the intellectually curious and inquiring. In embodying the values, purposes and mission of The Veritas Forum, Veritas Books provide thoughtful, confessional Christian engagement with world-shaping ideas, making the case for an integrated Christian worldview and moving readers toward a clearer understanding of ultimate truth.

www.veritas.org/books

Finding God at Harvard: *Spiritual Journeys of Thinking Christians*
edited by Kelly Monroe Kullberg

Finding God Beyond Harvard: *The Quest for Veritas*
by Kelly Monroe Kullberg

The Dawkins Delusion?: *Atheist Fundamentalism*
and the Denial of the Divine
by Alister McGrath and Joanna Collicutt McGrath

Finding Calcutta: *What Mother Teresa Taught Me About*
Meaningful Work and Service
by Mary Poplin

Did the Resurrection Happen? *A Conversation with*
Gary Habermas and Antony Flew
edited by David Baggett

A Place for Truth: *Leading Thinkers Explore Life's Hardest Questions*
edited by Dallas Willard

Is Reality Secular? *Testing the Assumptions of Four Global Worldviews*
by Mary Poplin